Reminiscences and Recipes

A COLLECTION OF MOSTLY MAINE MUSINGS

Barbara Rogers Jolovitz

Reminiscences and Recipes

ISBN 978-0-945980-49-0

Library of Congress Control Number: 2012944901

Cover photograph by Beverly Hallam, *Barbara's Dessert,* 2006

North Country Press

Unity, Maine

"A very important thing is not to make up your mind that you are any one thing."

Gertrude Stein

Acknowledgements and Preface

My friend Beverly Moeckler told me they didn't have stories like mine in Wisconsin and I should write them down. REMINISCENCES AND RECIPES is the result. A former English teacher, Beverly shortened sentences, transposed clauses and did all things all English teachers do. Howard scanned me her corrections. Karl Rogers, Debbie and John Barlock and Suzy Helmrich read the stories and encouraged me to keep at it. Lester got verbal readings. Suzy and John were very patient with me and my limited computer skills. Karl and Debbie tossed in incidents they remembered from growing up with or hearing about many of the subjects of the reminiscences. Kate Krukowski Gooding and Estha Weiner lead me into the world of publishing.

Several people have been mentioned for their contributions to society: Beverly Hallam and Mary-Leigh Smart for their Surf Point Foundation where artists will be able to live and work for a year; Constance McCatherine and Martin Silver for New York University's Silver School of Social Work and future McSilver Institute for Poverty and Practice; Lester Jolovitz and Ken Walsh for their concern for children, the Alfond Youth Center and Camp Tracy; Mark Bortman for his service to the People-to-People Civic Committee, his preservation of Boston's historic sites and his gifts of Americana to Boston University. Where possible, permission was asked to use their stories and to edit to their satisfaction.

Others have contributed to society in different ways: Ruth Mendall taught classic studies for 16 years in the Waterville school system; Mira Dolley taught French for 47 years at Deering High School in Portland; Ray Martan Wells and Nicholas Wells were devoted to protecting Provincetown's land, theater and arts; Mary Sottery's concern for the safety of school children crossing a six-way intersection was remedied by getting traffic lights installed; Mary also served in the Maine Legislature where her primary focus was on the environment and the protection of Maine's aquifers.

Writing about family and friends was a welcomed visit to the past. Their shared gifts have given me cause to reflect on how they influenced my life's journey.

Food played an important part of that journey. My parents' home was where family gathered and eating was always part of such gatherings. Food has always been more than just putting dinner on the table. Presenting it attractively was, and is, as important as it tasting good. Many taught me how to cook ethnic delights which became part of my catering and teaching repertoire.

The cover "Barbara's Dessert" is a photograph taken by Beverly Hallam when she and Mary-Leigh Smart gathered for lunch here with Director Hugh Gourley and some of his Colby Art Museum staff. The dessert was fresh pineapple sautéed in butter, brown sugar and rum, vanilla ice cream and raspberry sorbet topped with a walnut tuile. The cranberry glass is an antique dimpled tumbler. Beverly was immediate in her response to allow me to use her photograph and I am delighted to do so.

Everyone is sincerely thanked for their contribution in my life which has enabled me to write this book.

Barbara Rogers Jolovitz
Waterville, Maine
Summer, 2011

Table of Contents

Adirondacks

"Could you meet me for lunch to talk about a catering job?" We arranged to meet at a nearby Greek restaurant to talk about going to the Adirondacks for a reunion weekend with several of Miss Porter's School classmates. The lake compound my hostess's family owned included a large main cottage and several small cottages. I accepted the job and we worked out menus. Food had to be transported from Portland. I asked if there was telephone service there as I had to make a phone call each evening. "He can come." And, he did.

We left on a Friday morning for the five-hour drive during which time I learned about some of the women. One was nearly blind. The husband of another left her and their six children to marry a classmate. Lenny Dunne, former wife of Dominick Dunne, had multiple sclerosis and was in a wheelchair. She also suffered the loss of a murdered daughter. The renowned dress designer of the "shift," Lilly Pulitzer, could not make it.

After collective arrivals, Lester, along to help me, got involved in baggage delivery to assigned cottages. It was not your every day lawyerly thing to do, not that serving and bussing were.

I had prepared a "proper" tea for their arrival but as tea time passed, I suddenly realized it was not tea they wanted. A friend used to say: "It is five o'clock somewhere; time to drink." It was five o'clock there. Cocktails ended with lobster dinner at 7:00 p.m. Lester and I became quite amused at our roles which seemed to become "staff," including having to stay in the kitchen and go up the backstairs off the kitchen to quarters on the second floor.

The dining room table sat twelve. Walls were covered with photographs of family, some of the men in white wool tennis attire and women in long dresses sitting on bleachers viewing the games. The tennis courts and bleachers were still on the grounds in total disrepair. Also on the grounds was a building that housed huge boilers for doing laundry.

The next day went well with the friends off for lunch. Lester and I had use of a rowboat while they were gone. Dinner was at Lenny's cottage as it was a struggle for her to get to the main cottage. Lester and I decided it would be nice to have our dinner in the living room in front of a blazing fire. The stone fireplace was two stories high. We stayed until we heard voices which alerted us to go back to our kitchen.

The reunion broke up after Sunday breakfast with teary goodbyes and thanks to Lester and me. They decided they would gather the following year in California at Lenny's and she would have a special guest. They did and were overjoyed in the company of Robert Wagner. Lenny's household staff took care of cooking and serving but had she not had staff, we were ready to go.

Adult Education

Teaching adults to cook was fun. Unlike cooking demonstrations in the gourmet shops where there were usually 25 people, there were eight to ten. It was hands-on: students could work with me so it would also be a tactile experience.

I taught at the Jewish Community Center. Mrs. Godfrey, one of Portland's renowned bakers in her later 70's attended. Pâte brisée was going to be taught. She told me she had come as she had never been able to make a good pie crust. I was honored to have her in the class.

At a party I catered, Mrs. Godfrey told me how successful her pies had become. She brought a mohn kuchen to the hostess which was offered at dessert. It was a yeast pastry baked with a poppy seed filling. I asked Mrs. Godfrey if she would teach me how to make it. She was pleased to be asked and we set up a time.

We used the same dough as her recipe for pecan rolls in the Portland Symphony Cookbook which her daughter Batyah, a mezzo soprano with the Metropolitan Opera, had given for the book. A poppy seed filling was enhanced with raisins, preserves and lemon juice.

It was a wonderful sharing and we were both successful in each other's teachings.

Pâte brisée was taught to a different group. I brought chilled pastry made up earlier in the day. We would make the dough in class but use the chilled dough for the tarte au citron we were going to make.

Two ladies in the class came together. They enjoyed the classes and the class enjoyed them. I found one especially interesting. She had dyed black hair, black eyebrows drawn to perfect arches and wore bright red lipstick. We were ready to roll out the pastry and I asked her if she would like to do it. She was apprehensive but a good sport. As she took the rolling pin in hand, she asked if she could do what she always did at home before rolling out pie crust. "Of course." She crossed herself and started rolling.

And then there was the woman who ran towards me as I was going into a store: "I made your lemon curd and it tasted just like yours."

MOHN KUCHEN

½ pound butter, softened
½ cup sugar
3 eggs
½ cup sour cream
3 yeast cakes
1 tsp. salt
5-6 cups unbleached flour
1 cup milk

Filling:

1 can Solo poppy seed spread
¼ cup strawberry preserves
¼ cup white raisins, cut up
Juice and rind of ½ lemon
Combine

Butter, softened
Cinnamon and sugar

Cream butter and sugar. Add eggs, sour cream and yeast cakes. Beat well. Add salt to flour and alternately with milk until a soft ball is formed. Place in bowl, cover with plastic wrap and refrigerate 7-10 hours or overnight.

Divide dough into thirds. Roll out, spread with butter; sprinkle with cinnamon and sugar; let rest 15 minutes. Spread with poppy seed mixture. Roll up, place in buttered baguette pans, spread tops with butter, sprinkle with cinnamon and sugar. Let rise until they fill the pans. Bake in 350 degree oven until very brown.

A Passion for Meringues

"Salve amici amicaeque – I am a retread," said Ruth Mendall. When asked by the Headmaster of Coburn Classical School in Waterville if she would like to teach Latin, she responded she couldn't remember a word of it. Graduate courses at Tufts and a semester at the Virgilian Academy in Cumae, Italy prepared her to teach Latin. She also taught classical studies for 16 years in three Waterville area schools.

I met Ruth when we were docents at Colby College Museum of Art where we gave tours to school children. Docents also had to do a study of and write a paper about an artist. The paper was delivered to all the docents. Ruth had talked about her friend Dahlov Ipcar and displayed her animal paintings, sculptured fabric animals, and the children's books she had written and illustrated.

My paper, "A Man of Tea," was about Isamu Noguchi, his sculpture, his interest in the tea ceremony and his quest for his Japanese ancestry. His mother was not Asian. The paper was brief as I had a Public Broadcasting documentary film to show. It began: "Marianne Moore in an essay quoted Yoni Noguchi on Japanese poems." Yoni Noguchi, Isamu's father, was a Japanese scholar. Hearing Marianne Moore's name and fondness for her poetry, Ruth became immediately interested in my paper and Noguchi. A bond was formed between us.

Later years were not kind to Ruth. A lower leg was amputated. Being unable to adapt to a prosthesis, she took to her wheelchair and adapted her 1700's home to accommodate her needs. She managed to take care of herself with assistance from a neighbor. Family lived nearby.

Four of us docents maintained contact with Ruth. Alice, who had worked at the Museum keeping everything running smoothly, was retired and worked out lunch visits with Ruth to include Mary and Bonnie. We would bring lunch. After lunch, we shared our lives with Ruth and each other. Ruth always produced books she had read and felt we might like to read. We made notes as our guru spoke.

Ruth will be 96 in September (2011). She gave up her beloved home last year – "the two mice in the kitchen decided for me" – and lives in an apartment nearby. When I phoned her for my background information, she was delighted to be included and said, "Be sure to include my passion for meringues."

MERINGUES

3 egg whites, room temperature and free of any yolk
¾ cup sugar
Pinch salt
½ tsp. vanilla

Heat oven to 140 degrees. Line a cookie tray with parchment paper.

Place egg whites and salt in a dry, grease-free bowl. Using a whisk attachment of electric mixer, beat egg whites on low speed for 1 minute or until frothy.

Increase speed and whisk until the whites form stiff peaks, approximately 2-3 minutes.

Continuing to whisk, gradually adding the sugar. Beat approximately 2-3 minutes after all the sugar has been added. The mixture should look glossy and form long stiff peaks. Add vanilla and beat until just combined.

Using a large spoon, place free form shapes on cookie tray. Bake 30-40 minutes until the meringues are pale and dry. Turn off the heat and allow meringues to cool in the oven.

To prevent meringues from cracking, do not open oven door for the first half of baking.

Can be stored in an airtight container for up to a week.

Asparagus Properly Eaten

Summer berries swimming in cream with a square of her puff pastry lightly dusted with confectioners' sugar was the way May Rogers served blueberries a friend had dropped off or raspberries she had picked from her bushes. Her small cluttered kitchen was her domain preparing cream-laced clam chowder made from quahogs raked and shucked by her family. Sunday dinner was often leg of lamb served with traditional English mint sauce made from fresh mint she grew for the sauce. She was true to her heritage.

Standing in the doorway between the dining room and kitchen, I silently observed my mother-in-law as she whistled and prepared her forthcoming meal. I dared not interrupt with questions.

Afternoon tea was served with sweets she had baked earlier in the day. Often Ray and Nicky Wells would join us. Ray read everyone's tea leaves much to the delight of my children, Karl and Debbie. Talk would often go back to the old days when Ray summered in her shack on the dunes and her friendship with Eugene O'Neill. She also shared interest in food and the writings of Alice Waters and M.F.K. Fisher.

Dinner was colorful and always served on heated plates. Frequently asparagus were served. The technique of a spear being eaten with fingers was newly observed. I figured if May Rogers did it, it must be proper. It was.

She lived to be 80 without exercising and with salting all her cooking, albeit a bit much at times; she buttered her potato chips. But, she never smoked.

MINT SAUCE

Wash and dry mint. Pick leaves off stem. Chop leaves.

For 1 tbsp. mint, just cover with boiling water. Add ¼ cup sugar or to taste, ¼ cup cider vinegar.

PROVINCETOWN INDIAN PUDDING

3 cups milk, scalded

½ cup yellow cornmeal
¼ cup sugar
1 tsp. salt
1 tsp. cinnamon
½ tsp. ginger

1 egg, beaten
½ cup molasses

2 tbsp butter

1 cup very cold milk

Vanilla ice cream

275-300 degree oven. 1 ½ quart casserole, buttered

Scald milk

Combine cornmeal, sugar, salt, cinnamon and ginger. Stir cornmeal mixture slowly into scalded milk.   Stirring constantly, cook over low heat until mixture begins to thicken.

Mix egg with molasses. Blend a little hot cornmeal into the egg mixture to warm it; then add it to the hot cornmeal. Continue stirring and cook until thickened, about 15 to 20 minutes. Pour into casserole.

Add butter and stir until melted.

Pour 1 cup cold milk over top. Do not stir in.

Place in preheated oven, bake about 2 hours. A knife inserted in pudding will come out clean when done.

Serve warm topped with vanilla ice cream.

Variation: 2-3 peeled and chopped Granny Smith apples and ½ cup raisins can be stirred in just before pouring into casserole.

Before the Harpsichord

Paris has always been a magical mysterious place in our family as my uncle served in France in the First World War and he traveled to Paris frequently. He saw Edith Piaf singing on street corners. He spoke French fluently.

My cousin Betsy spoke French fluently. She was living in Paris for a year taking master harpsichord lessons to prepare for a competition in Bruges. A harpsichord was to be shipped to her from Boston which she would ship to Bruges for the competition.

"If you can come before the harpsichord, you are welcome. Bring sheets and towels." An invitation to visit Paris. Jean Miller would go with me.

I immediately got in touch with Mira Dolley to tell her the exciting news. Mira told us things to do in Paris and suggested the Loire Valley for touring. She would plan an itinerary. We would start at Chartres with its never replicated "Chartres blue" glass in its stained glass windows. We would visit castles, eat Bélon oysters, eat crêpe in Brittany and go to Mont St. Michel for overnight at Mère Poulard.

While in Paris, we went with Betsy to the William Dowd harpsichord factory. She showed us exquisitely decorated harpsichords done by a woman who had made a lifelong study of them. We left there for a café lunch of choucroute garni: sauerkraut with potatoes, sausage, onions, white wine and juniper berries. We picked up croissants and pastries for later indulging.

We visited the Louvre and the Impressionist museum L'Orangerie and felt the wonder of being close to painting seen only in books. We went to the Eiffel Tower and had tea at Angelina's.

A car was picked up in Paris. We started our touring at Chartres Cathedral. Its Rose Window and other stained glass windows were amazing as were its flying buttresses. Construction of Chartes began in the early 13th Century. Its treasured windows were removed during the Second World War. The Cathedral did not sustain damage during the war.

Our lunches were most often purchased at an outdoor market or a shop. They were usually cheese, charcouterie, baguette, white wine and a beautiful pastry to top it off. We lunched en plein air.

Bélon oysters were eaten in Bélon. In Brittany, we ate its traditional buckwheat crêpe served at dinner unfolded and covered with mushrooms and onions. We had them next day on a street corner cooked on a special stone. They were folded, slathered with butter and served in paper.

The end of our tour found us at Mont St. Michel, a rocky tidal island abbey which had been a pilgrim site from A.D.708 though monks had lived there since the 6th Century.

We were instructed where to park in the causeway to avoid the bore tide which traveled eight miles in and out with each tide. It was blustery walking to the town and around the 15th Century fortifications which surrounded Mont St. Michel. We settled in at Mère Poulard for the night. Dinner there included its famous omelet cooked in a long-handled sauté pan over a fire in a huge fireplace. The agneau de pré salé, salt meadow lamb, had its own particular flavor from the salt meadow grass upon which it fed.

Next day, ever curious Betsy led us through the foundations of the abbey. We ended up in a sunlit chapel. Betsy went to a music stand and said the music was a 10th Century Gregorian chant. "Would you like me to chant it for you?" Her chanting created an amazing feeling as I thought of where I was, listening to my cousin chanting music in this place created so many centuries ago. It has not been forgotten.

We returned to Paris, went to more museums and prepared to return to share with Mira our splendid trip with thanks to her and to Betsy who made it possible to visit before the harpsichord.

BUCKWHEAT CRÊPE

1 cup flour
½ cup buckwheat flour
¾ tsp. salt

4 eggs

1 cup milk
2 cups water
¼ cup butter, melted

Mix flours and salt. Add eggs; mix well.

Gradually add milk and water, stirring, until smooth. Stir in butter.

Let stand 20 minutes. Can be mixed in a blender or processor.

Mushrooms, sliced thin and sautéed in butter
Onions, sliced thin and sautéed in butter

Eggs, beaten

Sauté pan measuring 8 inches across the bottom.

Brush pan with melted butter or Canola oil. Heat pan on fairly hot burner (test by sprinkling a few drops of water which should sizzle when hot). Pour minus ¼ cup of batter into hot pan, tilting pan to cover bottom. Cook crêpe on one side; turn over. Spread some beaten egg, mushrooms and onions on top. Cook until egg is cooked to desired doneness. Slide onto warmed plate.

Stir crêpe batter between each crêpe. Brush pan with melted butter or oil between each crêpe.

Note: A knife gently slid under an edge of the crêpe when it looks done helps to release it before turning it over with a spatula.

Bonjour

Knowing I was going to Paris in the spring, I had four months to learn a few words in French. My high school French failed me and I it. I decided to take conversational French at the YWCA. The class was taught by Catherine Savell, a young French woman. Though I did not have high expectations in my ability to learn much, I did enjoy the class.

The next week, as I was going to my car, I noticed a young woman walking her dog. She looked familiar — "Aren't you the French teacher at the Y?" "Yes, I am." Catherine and her husband Geoff lived diagonally across the street.

Thus began a friendship which resulted in often cooking together. Her ability to cook so well at age 23 astonished me. She taught me how to make pâte brisée which resulted in making tarte au citron, tarte à la moutarde. We made pâte feuilletée, a puff pastry used for le pithiviere, an almond cream baked between two rounds of the pâte sealed together with a fluted edge. We also used it on a vol-au-von made with creamed seafood baked with a lid of the pastry. We made madelaine; we made clafoutis using her grandmother's recipe. Most fun was making couscous in a couscouserie to be used under a spicy beef concoction she prepared.

Catherine spent her growing up years in Ethiopia where her father was stationed with the United Nations. Her father was still in the service of the United Nations in Tangier, Morocco. Catherine was going to visit them, stopping off in Paris for a few days. She invited my daughter Debbie to join her. They would stay in Catherine's brother's apartment in Paris. Debbie recalled seeing the top of the Eiffel tower out of the kitchen window.

Being president of the Alliance Française, Catherine invited me to go to a meeting. I joined the group. Knowing I could contribute nothing to the language, my contributions of madelaine and tarte au citron to a meeting served me well.

We ultimately met Catherine's parents. It was easy to see where their daughter's charm came from. We called them Maman and Papa. For some reason I don't remember, Catherine came to the door one morning. As she was leaving, I asked her to give my regards to her parents. "I will tell them you said bonjour."

After Catherine and Geoff left Portland, they had three daughters and Catherine became a Professor at Loyola University in Maryland. We communicated for many years. All that she taught me as part of our shared cooking has remained with me and I am grateful to her for that and her wonderful smile.

APPLE GALETTE

One half recipe Pâte Brisée

5-8 Golden Delicious apples, sliced thin, using broken pieces and ends for the middle.
Chop broken pieces and ends.

Roll out pastry to about a 12-inch circle. Place on a round of parchment paper on the back of a cookie tray, or in a pizza pan.

4 tbsp. sugar
3 tbsp. butter
Apricot preserves

400 degree oven.

Place cut up pieces into the center of the pastry; overlap slices to within 1 ½ inch from the border. Sprinkle with sugar, dot with butter. Fold the 1 ½ inch of pastry over the apples. Sprinkle lightly with sugar. Bake ¾ of an hour or until nicely browned.

Apricot glaze.

Place ¼ cup apricot preserves in saucepan with a tablespoon of sugar. Heat, stirring, until sugar is dissolved. Spread on hot galette.

The galette is best if used the same day.

CLAFOUTIS LIMOUSIN MILLIARD

5 heaping tbsp. flour
3 heaping tbsp. sugar
Pinch salt
5 eggs
1 ¼ cup milk
2 cans dark cherries, drained
Butter

Sugar

400 degree oven. 9-inch deep fluted quiche dish. 25-30 minutes.

Combine dry ingredients. Beat in eggs, one at a time and well. Stir in milk.

Place cherries in buttered dish. Pour custard over cherries and dot with butter. Bake until risen, browned and center is set.

Sprinkle with sugar as soon as it comes out of oven.

PÂTE BRISÉE

1 -2/3 cup flour
Pinch salt
1 stick butter, chilled
3 tbsp. shortening

5 tbsp. ice water

Cut butter into flour and salt; add shortening. Lightly mix with finger tips until butter is about the size of peas.

Add ice water, combining with a fork until mostly combined. Place dough on a piece of plastic wrap and gather into a round, pressing out with palm of hand as gathering which will work in the butter a bit more. There should be some butter pieces remaining. Wrap. Refrigerate a few hours.

Roll out on floured parchment paper.

TARTE AU CITRON

One half recipe Pâte Brisée

400 degree oven. 9 inch tarte tin.

Roll out dough into a round, drape over rolling pin and fit into tarte pan. Prick bottom; chill for ½ hour. Line shell with waxed paper, fill with metal pellets or dry beans; bake in lower 1/3 of oven for 10-15 minutes or until set. Remove waxed paper, prick shell again; bake 10-15 minutes longer or until browned. Cool on rack.

Lemon Filling:

3 eggs
2/3 cup sugar
Juice and rind of 3 lemons

2 tbsp. butter

425 degree oven. 6 minutes

Combine all but butter in saucepan. Cook, stirring, over medium heat until thick. DO NOT BOIL. Stir in butter. Cool over ice water. Pour into cooled baked shell. Bake in upper 1/3 of oven 6 minutes.

Garnish with very thin lemon slices.

Cream Sauce

Aunt Rose was always in our lives. My sisters and I were the children she never had though she had more than one marriage. She had a wonderful sense of humor and could tell stories with a Yiddish flavor though often needing translation.

A professional entertainer, she played the accordion until breast cancer forced her to switch to the piano. One time when Esther and I were in Boston, we were fortunate to go with her on a job where she accompanied Ray Bolger. They hadn't rehearsed. All Aunt Rose needed was the name of the song and the key. She was a consummate musician who kept up with current music, playing it on either her baby Steinway or her organ beside the piano.

We loved Aunt Rose's tales. I especially liked the one about her marriage at fifteen. Her teacher in cooking class on what was Aunt Rose's last day of school told the class they would be making cream sauce on Monday. "I won't be here Monday." "Why won't you be here, Rose?" "I'm getting married." Her comment after telling the story was "I still don't know how to make cream sauce."

Knowing she was coming from Boston where she lived – "I love Boston" – we always anticipated the goodies she would bring: bagel, pumpernickel and herring from Harvard Street in Brookline; gallon jars of huge green olives from the North End, and Liederkranz cheese from a little gourmet shop on Dartmouth Street. It was the cheese my parents especially anticipated. The smell after it was unwrapped signaled it was time for Vivian, Esther, and me to leave the table.

Her visits also meant she would play the piano for us. "What would you like me to play?" The answer was always the same: "Humoresque and Swanee." She played them as one: Humoresque in the right hand; Swanee, the left. It always ended with a glissando and "what else." She knew what else and would immediately start playing silent movie music with a running commentary ranging from cops and robbers to our heroine tied to railroad tracks and saved by her lover just in time as the train bore down.

Although our dining room was small, it accommodated two upright pianos for future plans Aunt Rose had laid out for Esther and me: "Two beautiful twins, in two beautiful evening gowns, at two beautiful pianos." Such was not our fate; however, the pianos accommodated Aunt Rose at one and one of her siblings at the second much to the pleasure of all of us.

One time when Esther and I were in Boston, Aunt Rose felt it time we learned the facts of life. The best place for that would be the Old Howard, Boston's infamous strip tease theater in Scully Square. We were thirteen and we were educated.

Aunt Rose was a great cook, always making copious amounts of food. Rest assured, however, no matter what she cooked, she was true to her word. Nothing was served with cream sauce. She never learned how to make one.

BREAD PUDDING

1 quart milk
1 stick butter
1 cinnamon stick

1 loaf white bread, crusts removed, broken into pieces

6 eggs, beaten

1 tsp. vanilla
1 small can fruit cocktail

Carmelized pan

350 degree oven. Bake one hour.

Bring milk, butter and cinnamon stick to a boil. Remove from heat. Remove cinnamon stick.

Add bread to hot milk. Temper the eggs and then add to milk mixture; add vanilla and fruit cocktail. Mix well. Pour into carmelized pan. Bake.

Cool. Refrigerate. When ready to serve, run a knife around pudding and invert onto platter.

Dinah and Douglas Coyne

In the Maine Bar Journal, properties were advertised to entice lawyers to travel to Europe or exotic places. Lester saw an advertisement for a month in a house in Chipping Campden, England. Chipping Campden was in the Cotswolds, an area of narrow roads, charming villages, hedgerows and sheep in the meadows. We told a couple at the Colby College function about our plans. They asked if they could join us. We arrived in London, picked up our car and were on our way to Chipping Campden.

After settling into our house, we walked to town for lunch. As we were leaving, we saw a sign pointing to an art exhibit by Douglas Coyne. We were greeted by the artist and the first painting I saw was a pair of weathered boots. I liked it as I had photographed the pair of weathered boots I had been wearing all winter. Anyone who would do a painting of old boots… We worked our way around the exhibit and came to a table. We were greeted by a lady with round glasses, scarf on her head and welcoming smile. The lady was Mrs. Coyne. We chatted, told her about us and where we were staying. By the time we left them, they were Dinah and Douglas.

We would occasionally see Douglas in town but never Dinah. Late one afternoon, Lester and I were leaving the house for a walk and there they were. We walked with them and they invited us for coffee at their home the following week. The invitation was followed up by a note slid under the door confirming the date, time and location of their home. Arriving at the appointed time, we were given a tour of their gardens and then went in for coffee. I sensed an immediate friendship with Dinah. As we were leaving, I asked her if she would like to correspond. That was 18 years ago. Our correspondence is now by e-mail and we talk on birthdays and holidays.

Dinah was awarded an M.B.E. – Member of the British Empire – for her services to the Campden Voluntary Group which she founded. Its purpose was to "help people who were unwell or infirm." The award was presented to her by Queen Elizabeth.

Douglas taught graphic design at the Royal College of Art in London and he freelanced in graphic design as well. After he resigned, taking early retirement, he started to paint again. We are fortunate to have Douglas's watercolor of Dinah sitting in our home when they visited us 14 years ago.

They moved from Chipping Campden to Beckford, near Tewksbury. Douglas died there in April, 2009 and Dinah recently moved back to Campden. We continue sharing our lives as we have for so many years.

Doesn't the Governor Get Lunch

Many years ago, I catered a fundraising lunch in Cape Elizabeth for Massachusetts Governor Dukakis who was running for president. It was a perfect summer day. The setting of the home which faced the water and its lovely grounds enhanced the day. Lunch was to be spanakopita and Greek salad and would be served to the group. Debbie was with me to help serve.

When we got to the home, we were met by the Governor's advance man who informed us what was going to happen: "The Governor will be here at 11:45 and he will be here for exactly 45 minutes. He does not each lunch as his wife sends lunch with him." We had our instructions: the Governor would not be served lunch.

The Governor and his entourage appeared at precisely 11:45; he was greeted, hands were shaken and lunch was served. Debbie was busy serving and did not serve the Governor. He approached Debbie: "Doesn't the Governor get lunch?" Debbie came to me in the kitchen: "The Governor wants lunch."

He greeted guests, ate lunch, said a few words, thanked his hosts and was off to another fundraising event, all in 45 minutes.

Figs in Crystal

Summer. A client called to engage me to do a party to be held in their pool house. The foods were to be Italian. They must come from Boston's North End, the legendary Italian section of Boston.

We went to the North End. In addition to restaurants on every corner, there were purveyors of salamis, cheeses and barrels of green, black, pitted and/or stuffed olives and other traditional Italian condiments. Bakeries displayed stacks of pizzelle and pastries gaudy with colored icings and sprinkles. Jordan almonds were scooped from barrels. Fruiterers offered beautiful grapes and, most important, figs, perfect figs.

Returning from Boston and discussing the party, two specific requests were made: one was that the pasta salad would be made the Italian way with garlic and olive oil. Second, the figs were to be the centerpiece, piled high in a crystal bowl "the way we always served them."

It was done to specifications.

1985. Glasnost (Publicity). Mikail Gorbechev declares: "Russia will acknowledge the nation's social and economic problems, will have a more open government and a wider dissemination of information."

16 July, 1988. Frankfort, Germany. We were Missouri Tourin' Tigers, thanks to alumnus Donald Buxton. We were going to Russia with him, his wife Georgia and Dick and Joanna Dennis. Joanna was Georgia's sister. I had not met Donald and Georgia. After almost two weeks together, I got to know them and liked them very much.

Leningrad, also known as St. Petersburg, was to be our first stop. At a brief meeting at the airport with Gary from Tourin' Tigers, we were told we could not drink the water in Leningrad, not even use it for brushing teeth. Water could be bought at a market in the airport.

Upon arrival in Leningrad, we were herded into buses, taken to its small old airport to queue, present passports, visas and ourselves. A uniformed young man behind an enclosure examined our documents and us. It was very warm and would remain so throughout the trip. Divided into two busses, we were taken to our hotel and given room cards which had to be turned over to someone who gave us a key to our 10th floor room.

Peter the Great (1672-1725) became czar of Russia 1682 upon the death of his brother. He assumed control of the government in 1689. He established St. Petersburg in 1703 on territory conquered from Sweden. He attempted to reorganize the country on Western lines. He modernized the army, built a fleet, remodeled the administrative and legal systems and brought the church under State control. He visited Holland and Britain to study Western techniques and he worked in shipyards while there. He was ready to build his city in the delta of the Neva River. Using 100,000 peasants a year for nine years, he built 34,500 buildings and 350 bridges to span the Neva and canals.

There were five million people living in St. Petersburg. Trolleys plied the city of drab buildings in need of repair. Our 1,200 room hotel was built in 1918 by Russians and Swedes. We were in the "White Nights" of summer, a twilight glow past midnight. By four a.m., it was dawn, never having gotten dark.

Our touring began. We were taken to huge red columns with nautical statues at the bases. The columns were originally lighthouses. We faced an island which housed the Peter and Paul fortress. Its church had a distinctive tall and slender Dutch spire, the only spire of its kind. All the other 118 churches had the traditional onion tops and most had been converted into museums. The spire had been painted grey during the war and regilded in 1947. Looking east across the Neva, we saw the Winter Palace, its soft blue and white stucco and decorative gold known as Peter the Great baroque architecture.

The Hermitage. One of five palaces of the Winter Palace which housed over a million objet d'art and the library of Catherine the Great (1729-1796). A Lithuanian peasant, Martha Skavronsky married a Swedish dragoon and eventually became the mistress of Peter the Great. In 1703 she was rechristened Katarina Alexeievna. In 1711, Peter divorced his wife; married Catherine in 1712. In 1724, she was proclaimed empress.

St. Isaac's. Built by a French architect in 1818 in Classical style, it is 101 meters high and took 40 years to build. It is huge, weighs 300,000 tons and was built on 20,000 granite pilings. Its 10 ton carved wood and bronze doors are the largest in the world. The dome is the fourth largest in the world with St. Paul's dome in London being third largest. St. Isaac's was glorious. Its icons were mosaic with unbelievable shading. Pillars were malachite and lapis lazuli. A stained glass window of Christ appeared through partially opened doors. It was framed by lapis lazuli columns. There were pink marble columns of Corinthian order and topped in gold. St. Isaac's was closed and bombed during the 900 day siege. Restoration cost 2.5 million rubles.

We were taken to the battleship Aurora. In 1917, it fired blanks at the Winter Palace signaling the start of the Revolution. A museum since 1987, we were not allowed to board her.

The fortress of Peter and Paul was built in 1715-1733 as Sweden was constantly attacking the area. Peter built it as a political prison, never a fortress. His son Alexcy was plotting against him. Alexcy was the first to be killed there on orders from Peter. Alexcy, his sister, Peter and Catherine are buried there in tombs made from Carrara marble.

We were supposed to go to Yerevan at some point in the trip but uprising problems prevented it. We were told we will go "wherever there are beds."

Donald had a fascination with the brooms used by babushkas – old women – to sweep the streets. He decided he wanted one and took off early one morning to find one and he did. He amazed us.

There were kavas tanks everywhere. People queued for the drink made from rye bread and were fizzy, according to Gary. It was sold in a stein-type glass and after it was drunk, the glass was turned upside down, placed on a shelf, pressed down and it was sprayed with water. It was now "washed" and ready for the next customer. We did not drink kavas.

The next day, we hydrofoiled to Petrovorstz, Peter's Summer Palace. Built in 1703, there was an area built from the sea to allow boats to come directly to the palace grounds. We were not allowed that privilege and had to walk the distance to get to the palace. Fashioned after Versailles, it took 10 years to build. There were 180 fountains. Before we could enter the palace, shoe covers had to be put on. The floor in the lobby was squares of black and white marble. In the rooms, the floors were parquet; wall coverings and drapes were silk. The palace had been occupied by the Nazis (never "Germans") throughout the siege with restoration beginning immediately after they left.

Next day in the late afternoon, we were to fly to Tbilisi, Georgia's capital and largest city. Our plane briefing: take toilet paper; the bathroom smells terrible; air conditioning starts after the plane takes off; applause upon landing is not appreciated; the flight crew leaves before we do. The hotel green bagged dinners for our flight: 1 cucumber; 2 sandwiches each with a slab of cheese and salami; 1 hard-boiled egg; salt; a tart with jam, cinnamon and sugar.

As we waited to board our plane, we saw two women emerging from the plane. They wore white jackets over their short dresses, babushkas, white ankle socks and heavy black shoes. Each had a bucket and broom. They were the cleaning crew.

We finally boarded and eventually were given a tea bag, a cookie and three sugar cubes. Quite some time later, hot water in a bowl and a spoon was distributed and ready for the tea bag.

The airport at Tbilisi was lively with cars, taxis and lights. Our jovial bus driver had a cooler in the rear of the bus filled with cold beer.

Our bedroom was interesting. The wooded floor was a herringbone pattern; beds were single against-the-wall style with a mattress and thin pad. The bathroom had no shower curtain, a sink half off the wall, a non-working toilet and it smelled. The towels were a small hand towel and a bath towel measuring 3 feet long x 8 inches wide.

Georgians have their own language and alphabet. They originated from Spain, were dark complexioned with dark hair and dark eyes.

After dinner, we strolled the eight people wide sidewalks and decided to go into a pastry shop. A woman behind the counter took a jelly roll off a shelf, cut it into six pieces and presented it to Georgia. Standing on the corner eating the cake, we were approached by a man. He started talking with us and told us he taught English. He asked if we had any pens (we had been told to bring lots of pens). We gave him some. I had a small flashlight one squeezes to go on and gave it to him for his wife. He thanked me and in the same breath asked if I had any pens. He kissed the ladies hands and was off.

Joanna, Georgia and I went into a tea shop. As we were leaving, a clerk followed us out with three gift boxes of tea.

We noted at 10 p.m., it was just starting to get dark and people were still strolling. Young women wore very heavy black eye make-up. Women did not wear pants.

Next day, Lester was laid low with a cold and did not go to the farmers' market. Georgia and I were buying spices when a handsome woman came up to us and asked if we were Americans. She has been a ballerina with the Georgian Ballet and had danced in Boston and Chicago. She told us how to use the spices and bought three packages for us as "a gift from Georgia."

We travelled next day. Lester felt awful and was stricken with "quick trots." The roadside rest area was deplorable. Though we had Immodium with us, we visited a lady in the first seat of the bus who had something prescribed. She became the most popular person on the trip. Since there were now 14 in the same situation, we figured it was dinner the night before.

Lunch was in Gori, Stalin's birthplace. The 14 mentioned above were give yoghurt, rice and tea. Most important, however, there was a working restroom.

We spent the night in Tskalatubo and were amazed to see oleander, cactus and low palm trees. Our room had a civilized bathroom, no shower curtain but no odor either. The bottom sheet actually covered the mattress. We were waiting in the bus next day when an authoritative looking woman boarded. She asked who stayed in a certain room. Joanna said she had and was escorted off the bus. Seems as though Joanna had taken a towel to wrap something. The towel was retrieved from her suitcase, returned to the woman and we were on our way to Sochi on the Black Sea, 12 hours away.

We drove through mountains, narrow twisting roads, cars passing on curves, dense woods, cattle, pigs and goats in the road. We stopped for lunch at 3:00 p.m. and not daring to chance getting to Sochi until 9:00 p.m., I succumbed to a Turkish toilet. We arrived in Sochi at 6:00 p.m.

We were comfortable on the 4th floor. The stony beach in front of the hotel had to be reached by going through the hotel. People who wanted to swim in the hotel pool had to be examined by a doctor at the hotel before being allowed to swim.

There was a pavilion in front of the hotel with a sea of green benches covered with bikini-clad bodies sunning, sleeping, eating, playing cards. There was a latticed roof over the bodies offering a little protection from the sun. People came to this area fully clothed and stripped to their bikinis. The next day there was a trip to the tea plantation. We had an evening boat ride and prepared for tomorrow's two-hour flight to Moscow.

We arrived in Moscow late afternoon, seeing the Kremlin Walls and St. Basil's on the way to the hotel. Our room was quite civilized: a real bed, clean bathroom, hot and cold taps consistently reversed. Towels were good size.

There was a day early farewell party our first night. Lovely hors d'oeuvres of caviar in pastry cups, three-layered sandwiches of smoked fish, decorated with caviar or papaya and piped butter. Champagne and vodka flowed. After dinner, Lester, Joanna, Donald and Georgia decided to take the subway to Red Square. Dick and I declined as our stomachs were rebelling a bit. Lester said it was unbelievable, the guards at Lenin's tomb looked like wax figures, St. Basil's was gorgeous.

The next day we entered the Kremlin to visit the Armoury, built in 1480. The Fabergé eggs were on loan but the jewels, carriages, silver, gold, and Sevres china were not. The sleds were charming.

The three cathedrals in Cathedral Square were built about the same time as the Kremlin Walls, between 1485 and 1495. The 1733 czar bell, largest in the world, was on the ground. It got very hot in a fire and the water thrown on it cracked it. It had never tolled.

Magical St. Basil's was built in 1530. Its central dome was surrounded by eight cupolas, each dedicated to a saint when Ivan the Terrible won an important victory over the Tartars. In 1812, Napoleon stabled his horses in the church. In the evening, we attended a circus of horses, trained doves and bears. The moon was full and orange on our last night in Russia.

After lunch next day, our passports, visas and tickets were returned. A customs declaration form was filled out. Money and rubles were declared. No rubles were allowed out of the country.

August 28. We returned to Frankfort for an overnight and would return to America the next day.

Foods were not a memorable part of the trip. Most breakfasts were hard-boiled eggs and black bread waiting on every table. Sometimes sweet buns and yoghurt cheese were offered. Always available was apple juice, coffee and tea.

Lunches were most often an appetizer followed by soup. One soup I especially enjoyed was Salyanka: cabbage, finely diced carrots, potatoes, meat, fresh basil and parsley and sour cream.

Dinners were an appetizer of a salad and bread. Most entrées were meat which was most often very greasy. The gatherings of the Tourin' Tigers were very nice and usually caviar, smoked fish and blini were served as well as champagne, wines and vodka.

This story is from notes and the only one using notes. We were there shortly after glasnost so the Russians made efforts to accept us. The Georgians did not have to try – they were innately friendly.

We were most fortunate to have gone to a very different world from its towels to its caviar.

BLINI

1/3 cup buckwheat flour
2/3 cup flour
½ tsp. baking powder
¾ tsp. salt

1 egg
1 cup milk
1 tbsp. clarified butter

Combine dry ingredients

Combine liquids. Add to dry ingredients.

Sauté one tablespoon batter in clarified butter, spreading batter slightly; turn when browned to cook other side.

Top with:

Smoked salmon
Crème fraîche, sour cream or Greek yoghurt
Finely chopped red onions
Capers
Sprig of fresh dill.

Note: Blini pans are available in gourmet food shops.

Goodbye, Friend

"Could you stop by Friday afternoon about three?"

"Of course."

It was Ruthie Brandwein for whom I had catered and done food demonstrations in Sterns, her department store in Waterville. I knew she had not been well in recent years fighting cancer.

She greeted me at the door and led me into her den. "I want you to cater my funeral. It is to be the same as if it were a party," and she went on to tell me the foods she wanted, etc. A check had been written before I got there. We continued with small talk. We cried and hugged. She saw me to the door and another hug was our goodbye as we did not, could not speak.

Ruthie died a few weeks later and her goodbye to her mourners was exactly as she had wished but the key ingredient was missing.

MUSHROOMS IN GARLIC SAUCE

3 tbsp. olive oil, divided
2 cloves garlic, minced
1 ½ tbsp. flour
1 cup beef broth
½ dried red chili pepper, seeded and cut into 3 pieces
2 tbsp. minced fresh parsley, divided
2 tsp. lemon juice

½ pound small mushrooms

Heat 2 tbsp. oil over medium-high heat. Add garlic and sauté until golden. Remove from heat; stir in flour, mixing until smooth. Return to heat; cook 1-2 minutes. Gradually add broth; blend in chili pepper, 1 tbsp. parsley and lemon juice. Stir until smooth and thickened. Remove from heat and set aside.

Heat remaining oil until very hot. Add mushrooms and stir fry until lightly browned. (Can be made ahead to this point. Refrigerate sauce and mushrooms separately.) Add mushrooms and simmer 5 minutes. Serve sprinkled with remaining parsley.

TORTELLINI WITH PARSLEY-CAPER SAUCE

½ pound cheese tortellini

2 tbsp. parmesan cheese
1 clove garlic
2 tbsp. walnuts
2 tbsp. capers
¾ cup Italian parsley
Salt
Pepper

½ cup olive oil

Cook tortellini about 8 minutes or until done.

Process remaining ingredients except olive oil. Gradually add olive oil.

Pour sauce over tortellini. Mix well

Goodbye to Childhood

"I saw a woman on Congress Street who was so stunning I turned around to continue looking at her. I couldn't believe it when I met her that evening." My mother was talking about Madelaine Gordon. My parents met Madelaine and Nick Gordon that evening at my aunt's house.

Madelaine was from Texas. A tall woman with black hair pulled away from her face, small black eyes and a slight split between her top middle teeth. She was not beautiful. She was simply fascinating and she fascinated me, a 10-year-old child. She had a wonderful smile and her eyes closed when she laughed which she did often. Nick was an enigma. He had been a New York lawyer whose background was sketchy, information a child picks up when adults discuss such issues and think a child is not close enough to hear. Nick was older than Madelaine who may have been in her late 30's.

They lived in Portland and ran a hotel in Saco. They adopted Ricky who I used to babysit. When Ricky was five or six, they moved to Kinney Shores beyond Old Orchard Beach and we would visit them on a Sunday.

Madelaine was many "firsts" in my life: first to wear pants which billowed as she walked; first to sew all her clothes; first to make lasagna. As I was always in her shadow, I saw her take the lasagna out of the oven. It was beautiful. All bubbly and ringed with browned sausage, something I had never eaten – another first. I can see it now in its restaurant-size pan, large enough to feed a multitude.

Madelaine was my idol. I wanted to be just like her. My fascination for her never diminished over the years. Several years ago, I spent three days with her in Miami, the first time I had seen her since my teens. Having suffered a stroke, she was in a nursing home. I am not sure she knew me at first and, of course, would not have recognized me, but she smiled as though she did. It didn't matter. I had not forgotten her and I wanted to be with her. I was touched to see a picture of my twin sister Esther and me on her bulletin board of family faces.

Madelaine died about a year after our visit. My parting hug with her was the end to a wonderful chapter of my childhood.

"It's Hotham"

A house was going up on the street Lester had been developing over the years so we thought we would check it out. It was framed up and concrete was to be poured by Hotham Concrete. A burley smiling fellow and his young son came over to the car. "I'm Larry Hotham."

Lester said, "I knew Tiny Hawtham." "It's Hotham. He was my uncle." Lester in an aside to me said Tiny was not tiny. Lester continued his conversation with Larry, telling him he had been an Associate Judge of the Waterville Municipal Court for 16 years. "Oh, then you knew lots of Hothams."

Larry left to check on his crew and returned to tell us he grew up in the woods and returned as often as he could. He further told us the son who was with him was always helping him, that his brother was a better student and not with him as much. He suggested Lester would sell more lots if some of the trees were cleared out so people could see into the lots. He would be glad to clear them for the trees. It was agreed he would clear the lot next to where he was working as his equipment was there. The cleared lot remains just that.

Our last meeting with this delightful fellow had him telling us a lot of people called the Hothams Hawtham. At his father's funeral, the clergy who officiated referred to his father as Mr. Hawtham at which time one of the mourners yelled out, "It's Hotham."

Larry Hotham and his son left us to walk down the street to their truck.

Jacking Worms

Lester and Pat were talking about night crawlers and Lester said they used to "jack them." "Jack worms," I said. "Never heard of it in the city." They insisted one would go jacking worms.

I thought my son-in-law John from Houlton would know about jacking worms. Houlton is kind of remote in "the County." "Never heard of it. Even though I am from 'the County,' I was still a 'townie' and not a 'country boy.' So I guess I qualify more as city folk (we had cable TV!)"

When John's childhood friend Matt came over for the cookies I had made him, I brought up the jacking issue. "Have you ever heard of jacking worms?" "No. But when you hunt deer at night and you shine a light on them, they stop dead in their tracks. It is called jacking. A term from the early 1900's. I guess the term was applied to night crawlers which are found by flashlight. I don't know if they stop when a light hits them but you have to be quick to get them before they go back into their hole."

My hairdresser is a Waterville native. I knew she fished so I thought I'd ask her. "Claire. Have you ever heard of jacking worms?" "Oh, sure. When you jack worms, you are looking for night crawlers with a flashlight. You have to snatch them very quickly or they will go back into their hole. They jack deer too by shining a light on them. When I was a kid, I used to jack frogs. They'd come out from under the cottage at night. We would turn on the spotlight and they would head back under the cottage. They were fast. I had to work fast to get them and would put them in a pail. When we fished with them, I would put the hook under its lower jaw and their legs would go all over the place. They were really live bait."

That's jacking worms. And frogs.

Julia and Jacques

She flipped potatoes into the air, fully intending to catch them in the pan from which she flipped them. When they missed, she smiled and said, "If this happens..." She proceeded to gather the pieces, put them back into the pan and continued. She didn't panic and didn't miss a beat. That was my first viewing of Julia Child. If she could do that on television, I had no worries – anything could be patched up. I sensed a treasure had entered my psyche.

My quest for mastering Julia's art of French cooking continued as I tried her recipes on my family. We enjoyed coq au vin, ratatouille and boeuf bourguignon. I reversed crème renversée au caramel. We devoured Reine de Saba. I was French cooking. I never had to patch as I never dared to flip.

I was most fortunate in finding "Mastering..." for $2.00 at a garage sale. Scrutinizing the woman running the sale, I wondered why she would part with such a treasure and I felt sorry she gave up on French cooking.

Several years later, enter Jacques Pépin, my second teacher. Jacques never had to repair. He taught me more French cooking and how to decorate foods. Watching one particular show on how to make and decorate pâté, I thought it would be nice for catering and got an opportunity to try it out.

A hearty hors d'oeuvre cocktail party in Cape Elizabeth would be the place. Eggs were hard boiled to get whites for flower petals and yolks for centers. Green onions were blanched to make them soft to slice and bend to make graceful slender stems for the flowers and to cut into diamond shapes for leaves. Tomatoes were blanched to remove the skins; the flesh was for flowers. The decoration was sealed with aspic. It came out not quite Pépin but I was proud of it and felt it could be served.

It made it to the party and pleased my hostess as it was not your everyday pâté. However, no one ate it. As I was tidying up during the party, the conductor of the Portland Symphony Orchestra sought me out and said, "Your pâté is too pretty to eat." With that, we went to the pâté. I broke into it, spread some on cocktail bread, served him and left him on his own.

When people ask who taught me to cook, I unhesitatingly say Julia Child and Jacques Pépin. The two of them prepared me for catering.

CRÈME RENVERSÉE AU CARAMEL

Caramel

½ cup sugar
½ cup water

Boil sugar and water together until desired caramel color. Pour into pan, rotating pan to coat with caramel. Set aside.

Custard

3 eggs
1/3 cup sugar
2 cups milk, scalded

1 tsp. vanilla.

350 degree oven. Bake 40-45 minutes in a water bath.

Beat eggs and sugar lightly. Slowly add hot milk, stirring: add vanilla. Strain into caramelized pan.

Set custard into a large pan. Pour hot water into pan halfway up custard pan. Bake.

Remove from water bath to cool. Refrigerate until cold or overnight.

Run knife around custard to release. Invert onto a serving plate.

REINE DE SABA

350 degree oven
1 8-inch round pan, buttered and floured

4 ounces semi-sweet chocolate
2 tbsp. coffee
Melt chocolate in the coffee.

1 stick butter, softened
2/3 cup sugar
3 eggs, separated
Pinch salt
1/3 cup ground almonds
7/8 cup flour
3 egg whites
2 tbsp. sugar

Cream butter and sugar well. Beat in yolks. Stir in chocolate mixture, then flour and almonds.

Whisk whites until they hold their shape. Beat in the 2 tbsp. sugar. Stir some of the beaten whites into the batter; fold in remaining whites.

Turn batter into prepared tin. Bake about 25 minutes. Cool.

Icing:

½ cup semi-sweet chocolate
1 ½ tbsp. rum or coffee
Melt chocolate in rum
6 tbsp. butter, softened
Beat in butter until smooth. Ice cake.

July 23, 2011

I do not want to forget the date. Ray Martan Wells died on that date. She was 103.

After my potential in-laws, the first to look me over 56 years ago in Provincetown were Ray and Nicky Wells.

One could not say just "Ray." It was always RayandNicky. One word. But, there were years before Nicky.

Ray came to Provincetown in summers as a teen, living in a shack on the dunes where she could write, paint and live as she wished. She could visit with Eugene O'Neill as he also lived on the dunes. She would come to town for her mail and met my father-in-law at the Post Office where he worked. He introduced her to the family.

Theatre was her major focus. She was one of the co-founders of the Provincetown Theatre. She wrote scripts and spent time in Hollywood. In 2008, she was given the Lifetime Achievement Award by the Theatre.

She grew up in New Jersey going to the same high school at the same time as Nicky. However, they did not know each other. They met and married several years later. Ray introduced Nicky to her Provincetown. They were in the construction business in New Jersey but the pull to Provincetown was strong. They settled there buying the Charles Hawthorne home and immediately started renovating. Charles Hawthorn, influenced by William Merritt Chase, started the Cape Cod School of Painting and was a founding member of the Provincetown Art Association. The home had a commanding 360 degree view of the dunes, the harbor and Cape Cod Bay. Ray and Nicky started buying and renovating property to make art galleries. They opened "The Inn at the Mews," a restaurant overlooking the harbor.

They joined the Town Council and any group working for the betterment of the town. They were adamant the land and harbor would be protected.

Ray was dramatic; Nicky was not. Both were kind and caring. They always visited when we were in Provincetown and brought magic into our lives. Karl and Debbie loved being around them. Though Nicky died many years ago, they were in constant touch with Ray. Grandson Nicky is named for Nicky.

In declining health, Ray moved to New York City to be near her sister. Karl and Debbie saw her two years ago. They knew, as did Ray, it was their farewell.

The last time I saw Ray was at my marriage to Lester. After the usual speeches, Ray called out, "Let's hear from the bride."

The death of Ray brings an end to living associations with Provincetown. Only memories exist now, fascinating incredible memories. Karl, Debbie and I bid you adieu, RayandNicky.

Post Script, June 6, 2012.

On March 20, 2012, Ray's shack, known as the Nicholas and Ray Wells Dune Shack, became part of the National Register of Historic Places, Dune Shacks of the Peaked Hill Bars Historic District. The shack and 50 acres were originally purchased by Ray from Carlotta Monteray, Eugene O'Neill's wife.

Les DeMoiselles D'Avignon

Mira Dolley and I did not like each other. She, head of the French Department at Deering High School in Portland where she taught for 47 years, was my French teacher. I was a terrible student which made for an automatic clash.

Going ahead 30 years, I was reintroduced to Mira through Jean Miller. Jean and Isabel Pease were friends as student-teacher at Deering where Miss Pease taught English. Jean wrote poetry and belonged to a writers group Isabel put together. Isabel and Jean remained friends. Isabel and Mira were friends; thus, as a friend of Jean's I was accepted into the fold.

It was an experience of a lifetime knowing and learning from Mira. Her stories went back to Raymond where she was born, to France and beyond. Isabel's knowledge of art was generously shared. Both loved music. Isabel played the violin in the Portland Symphony Orchestra. Combined interests led us to music at Tanglewood, art at nearby Sterling and Francine Clark Art Institute and the Boston Museum of Art.

Mira loved to tell stories and her sense of humor and embellishments made for great listening. She talked about a cousin who was "a rather large woman" and was "like a frigate under full sail" as she walked the length of the church to her front row pew.

Winters found Mira living in Portland. She summered at the family homestead in Raymond, 45 minutes west of Portland. She would invite Isabel, Jean and me to Saturday night "suppah" of hot dogs, brown bread and her delicious baked beans cooked overnight in her kerosene fed stove.

Mira was especially proud of her Gilley Scholarship which allowed her to live a year in France. To be eligible for the scholarship, she had to document her ancestry for five generations in America. Stipulations were that she would travel France and not speak

English. If she was in Paris on a Sunday, she did indulge in the English edition of The New York Times.

College found Mira at Colby, graduating in 1919. In 1937 she was elected a trustee and received a Colby Brick in 1959 for services to the college. Lester graduated Colby in 1939 so he and Mira shared their professors and stories of the old campus.

Gertrude Stein was a favorite of Mira's. She took it upon herself to champion "Gertie." She lectured about Stein's life in Paris, her writings and the work she and Alice B. Toklas did during the War. She ended her lectures with a Stein reading. Mira willed to me her Stein collection. Her shards of paper markings as well as three pressed yellow pansies are as I received them.

Mira shared her family with us. On one birthday, Jean, Isabel and I took her to Bangor so she could lunch with her favorite cousin Charlotte Clement. Charlotte was the daughter of the "frigate under full sail" woman. Charlotte and her doctor husband ran an inn many years ago at Seal Harbor which Mira visited very often. Her nephew Steve told me that Seal Harbor was originally called Clement. Wanting a little more information, I contacted Bob Pyle, Director of the Northeast Library. He told me all the villages were named for the first settlers going back to the first decade of the 19th Century. The first Clement was a cooper. Steve and his wife Martha remain our friends. When they came to Maine from California to spend a few weeks in Somes Sound on Mount Desert, Lester and I would overnight with them, regaling ourselves in Mira stories or an "as Mira would say."

Mira, Isabel, Jean and I went to Europe for a month, arriving in Paris, on to Venice, Florence and Geneva. We lunched in Geneva with one of Mira's Deering students who was a translator. She thought the place for lunch should be the train station as they had "the best tête de veau." It almost did Isabel in as her eating habits were very simple, pushing the truffles aside which came with her lunch.

Mira, Isabel and Isabel's sister often travelled to Europe. They always visited France. On one of their trips, Mira called to reserve hotel rooms: "Madam, how will I know you?" "You will know us. We are three women and not Les Demoiselles d'Avignon," Picasso's painting of five nude women.

Wintering with Debbie and me for three years were winters of joy, learning and sharing. The evening I was to bring her to Portland, she suffered a stroke and was in a nursing home for several years. She died in 1994 in her 97th year.

Louise Nevelson

The last paper to be delivered by me to the docents at Colby College Museum of Art was in 1999. It was about Louise Nevelson. I had the winter to write it. As I became involved with her life, I decided the only way to present her was to be her. The paper would be written in first person. I would deliver it dressed in layers to look somewhat like a "collage" as she referred to the way she dressed. I would wear false eyelashes though not as caterpillarish as hers. Louise grew up in Rockland and since the Farnsworth Museum in Rockland had the second largest collection of her work, its docents were invited to attend.

I had the benefit of incidents relating to Louise from people who knew her. Hugh Gourley, Director of the Colby Museum, told me about a party the night before Louise and Bette Davis were to receive honorary degrees from Colby. Bette, who arrived late and tried quietly to leave early, was spotted by Louise who said in a loud voice to call attention to Bette's departure: "She is just so beautiful." Louise would never be outdone. Hugh was at a dedication of Louise's sculpture in New York which was being moved from Park Avenue to Central Park. He said she was dressed in a beautiful ankle length chinchilla-lined paisley coat worn with her old work boots.

Louise was honored by being invited to show her work at the 31st Venice Biennial in 1960. Beverly Hallam told me the Italian Government allowed her to photograph the entire show. Mary-Leigh recorded the shots, dates and technical data of every piece. Louise displayed in three galleries: a gold, a white and a black. Twelve new environments were composed for the event. Louise did not win but was highly praised by Giacometti who did win as did most Italian entrants.

My friend Charlotte Gordon lives in Rockland. She was the best friend of Louise's sister-in-law. Charlotte told me the story of Louise going away for a long weekend with a mutual friend. They were to meet at the station. Louise arrived without any luggage. Asked about it, she told her friend she was wearing all the clothes she would need.

My Aunt Rose was a friend of Louise's sister Anita who lived in Rockland at the Thorndike Hotel owned by their brother. Aunt Rose, Anita and I attended a luncheon in Louise's honor at the Farnsworth Museum. After lunch, I went to Louise, standing alone, to congratulate her. She was multi-layered, her hair wrapped in a flowing scarf, and, of course, thick lashes. Anita and Aunt Rose would sometimes go to New York for Louise's parties. I never asked about them.

In 2009, Alice Fitzgerald, who had been in charge of the Museum office, was now retired and a docent. She called to tell me Colby docents were going to do a symposium on sculpture. Someone at the formative meeting asked, "Do you think Barbara Jolovitz would be Louise again?" Louise came to life again for Colby, Portland Museum of Art and Bowdoin docents and my family.

This past winter, the Naples (Florida) Museum of Art installed "Dawn's Forest," 10 monumental white sculptures. Gifted from Georgia-Pacific and MetLife in Atlanta to the Naples museum, it was the first time "Dawn's Forest" was in a museum setting. It had been installed in Atlanta in 1980.

I did two performances in Naples. One was for a group studying Jewish women in the arts. The other was for a group taking an art class in sculpture. They would view the installation in the atrium and then gather outside. Louise would visit them there. It was very exciting to think about "Dawn's Forest" in back of me as I did my presentation.

Louise led what one might think was an exotic life but, in fact, she struggled in her personal and artistic life. She knew from childhood she wanted to be an artist and spent her life working to attain that goal. She paved the way for women artists. She worked hard, lived hard and died hard, ill for months with brain cancer. She died April 18, 1988. She was 88 years old.

At the end of the paper, I quote an interviewer asking Louise how she felt about reincarnation and if so, what would she like to come back as: "I don't believe in reincarnation but if I did, I would like to come back as Louise Nevelson."

Mark Bortman: 1896-1967

Born in Rumania in 1896 and immigrating to Boston with his parents in 1904, Mark Bortman's education included Boston University, Suffolk Law School and M.I.T. Mr. Bortman's business was waterproofing material to be used in the manufacturing of baby pants. I was his secretary for two years and Anna Fopiano was his bookkeeper. The office was on Essex Street, a block up from South Station. It was large enough to house some of Mr. Bortman's passion for Americana which included a handsome highboy with its dovetailed drawers, hand-fashioned drawer pulls, bonnet top and finial. Its provenance was that it came from the first person killed in Concord in the Revolutionary War. There were other handsome highboys but they did not have provenances. I used to polish the furniture using a recipe from the Boston Museum of Art. Mr. Bortman and his roll-top desk were in a small inner office.

Diaries from the Revolutionary War period were also collected. I transcribed them into modern English. A Boston University professor friend of Mr. Bortman's came to the office to translate them for me. Diaries were continually being bought so I was kept busy.

The Boston National Historic Sites Commission office was visited a couple afternoons a week. As its president, he and his commissioners saved Faneuil Hall from destruction in the early 1970's.

The original Faneuil Hall was built in 1742 by wealthy merchant Peter Faneuil. It had an open ground floor for merchants and an assembly room above. It was destroyed by fire in 1761 and rebuilt in 1762. In 1805, Charles Bulfinch, a famous architect in the Boston area, increased the size of the building and added more floors.

The original copper grasshopper weathervane was moved to the cupola on the newly expanded area.

The grasshopper has its own history. Suspected spies were asked to identify the object on the top of Faneuil Hall. If they answered correctly, they were freed; if not, they were convicted as British spies. The same grasshopper remains atop Faneuil Hall.

Mr. Bortman had a collection of Paul Revere silver. In 1948, Mr. and Mrs. Bortman donated over 2000 early Americana manuscripts and artifacts to Boston University. It included their Paul Revere silver collection. I had to deliver four pieces of Mr. Bortman's Revere silver to Boston University. It was another historic ride only this time by taxi.

Known for his Paul Revere collecting, in 1949 Mr. Bortman was asked by Israel Sack, a pre-eminent Boston dealer in American antiques, to assist in purchasing a Paul Revere bowl from its owner who was willing to sell the bowl, but only to a museum At the time, the Boston Museum of Art wanted the bowl but did not have the funds to purchase it. Feeling the bowl belonged in Boston, Mr. Bortman took on the task. The funds raised by public subscription and Boston school children bought The Liberty Bowl, as it was called, for $52,500. It was presented to the Museum. The bowl is the only piece of silver which commemorates the birth of a nation. The Liberty Bowl, the Constitution and the Declaration of Independence are considered the nation's most cherished historic treasures.

President Eisenhower appointed Mr. Bortman chairman of the People-to-People Civic Committee. The appointment required Mr. Bortman to be in Washington and Europe to promote a cultural understanding throughout international communities. The Sister-to-Sister program was established under the Civic Committee whereby an American city established a relationship with a foreign city. The program continues to the present. A Saville Row exponent, he always stopped in London for his bespoke three-piece suits when he traveled to Europe for the Civic Committee.

A member of the Ancient and Honorable Artillery Company, Mr. Bortman marched in the annual Patriot's Day parade. The Artillery Company was founded in 1683 and is the oldest chartered military organization in the Western Hemisphere. It exists today and maintains the 4th floor in Faneuil Hall.

The last time I saw Mr. Bortman was in 1958. I visited him to show off two-month-old Karl, the reason for my leaving Mr. Bortman's employ.

Mr. Bortman collected Americana to make sure it survived. He, in turn, gave it to Boston University which guaranteed its survival. He served his adopted country well and became a true American patriot.

Mc Catherine Silver: McSilver

Harry and Martha McCatherine summered next to my summering family at Little Sebago. Their daughter Connie, her husband Marty and their miniature Yorkshire terrier Gladys would visit them in August. All of us loved Harry and Martha. My daughter Debbie had a special fondness for Harry as he taught her to swim and to dive off their dock. Harry died several years ago; Martha died two years ago in her 99th year. Gladys has been replaced by other terriers but not forgotten – Marty's wooden boat is "Gladys." Connie and Marty and terriers continue their August at Little Sebago.

Connie and I shared unfortunate incidents with Mira Dolley at Deering High School in Portland. Connie, a 1957 graduate, was advised by Mira, Dean of Girls, that she should "be a secretary" and not go to college. That advice took Connie to New York where she worked for a New York airline. She met Marty the first week she was in New York. One might argue that Mira's advice was a blessing in disguise as Connie and Marty celebrated their 50th wedding anniversary this year.

In her mid-thirties and never having had the fulfillment of college, Connie's social worker friend 30 years her senior urged her to study social work at New York University. Connie got her B.S. in Social Work in 1978, M.S.W. in 1979, PhD. in 1983.

Marty grew up in the Bronx. He served in the army in Korea and under the G.I. Bill, he attended NYU's School of Commerce, graduating in 1958. Working as a stock broker early in their marriage, he ultimately became involved in a plasma collection business. The company grew to become one of the leading firms of its kind in the world.

Two years ago, Marty had surgery for cancer. Connie's nursing and devotion, together with chemotherapy, radiation and a feed tube were the winning combination.

Back to Little Sebago for the month of August, Marty and his garden of August blooming flowers are blooming mightily.

Connie taught at the School of Social Work at NYU. In 2003, she was appointed to the NYU Board of Trustees. In 2007 with a feeling of gratitude towards the school that enabled her to achieve the college education she had wanted for so long, Connie and Marty pledged $50 million to the NYU School of Social Work. It was the largest private donation to a school of social work in the United States. The school was renamed the Silver School of Social Work at NYU. Said Connie: "It is one of the greatest pleasures of my life to help the School of Social Work and Martin is proud to be able to offer his support to the School as well." The funds also will help lay the groundwork for a planned McSilver Institute for Poverty Policy and Practice.

Connie and Marty winter in Florida where Connie had been involved with the Indian Creek Village Public Service Department in mental health and social work, including training police officers in hostage negotiation, the dynamics of stalkers, and police suicide. In 1993 the National Association of Social Workers presented her with the Diego Lopez Award for Private Practitioners for her work with AIDS patients.

Their achievements away from Little Sebago have been monumental. Part of their gift will be used to support the Constance McCatherine-Silver Fellowship which provides financial aid to M.S.W. students in need who are dedicated to helping minority populations; to establish an endowment professorship for a junior faculty member researching poverty; and to promote other new initiatives dedicated to the study of poverty and to better allocate funding, administration, and services.

I have known them for so many years as members of the blueberry pie gang. Their achievements and their gift to NYU for the benefit of those who will help society is a profound legacy.

It has been a pleasure for me to write about Connie and Marty. It has been nice revisiting Harry, Martha and Gladys too.

Oslo to Loxley

August 24, 1997. Paul and BettyAnn celebrated their 50th anniversary. Lester and I celebrated our wedding. The next day, the four of us were going to Norway for a week and then to Loxley, England for three weeks. The Jensons wanted to visit the land of their ancestors and eat genuine lutefisk. A few weeks in England would be nice as we all loved England.

We were met in Oslo by Paul's former colleague and her husband who took us to our hotel. We would see them in a couple of days. They suggested we visit the 80-acre Frogner Park which contained a sculpture garden. The sculptures were the work of Gustav Vigeland. The most spectacular piece was a monolith of 121 human figures carved from a block of granite. Near our hotel was the building where the Nobel Peace prize was awarded.

We went to lunch with Paul's friends and spent the rest of the afternoon in their home. Next day we were off on the bus tour of Norway.

The first stop was a recreated village we walked around. Lunch was waiting for us at a farm house. After that, we were on our way to dinner and overnight in mountains. Statues of trolls were in front of homes all along the way. Morning departure was foggy. As we listened to Grieg's Piano Concerto during the descent from the mountain, one could sense the influence of Norway in his music.

We zigzagged our way up and down mountains, stopping at villages. Our guide told us at one church we visited that Norwegians were not religious. "We match them, hatch them and dispatch them." In other words they went to church on three occasions: weddings, christenings and funerals.

We did a water cruise staying at a hotel facing fjords and seven waterfalls. Lunch at the end of the cruise was goat meat. The last day of the tour, our driver treated us to aquavit before we descended the final mountain. He did not imbibe. We returned to Oslo to be on our way to England the next day.

London was in chaos as Princess Diana had been killed that day. Flowers were everywhere. Busses were off schedule and we waited three hours past our departure time. Dropped off at the wrong place, we finally made contact with our car rental place. We were on our way to Loxley. Paul would drive and I would navigate from the back.

We were pleased with our accommodations which Paul had found in a publication listing a variety of rental properties. Especially nice was having a laundry machine, one thing less for us to travel to as the only business in the village was a pub. Provisions had to be bought about 25 minutes from "home." The owners lived on the property and had horses in the fields beyond a fence. Their land was also leased for sheep to graze.

Lunches were usually eaten out so light suppers of soup and a sandwich would be sufficient. We became soccer fans though we didn't know a bit about the game; it was all we could get on the television.

Stratford-Upon-Avon was 40 minutes away. We picnicked one day beside the Avon, took a boat ride on the Avon and ate at Lambs on Sheep Street. The play we saw at the R.S.C. theatre was, unfortunately, not Shakespeare.

I had clipped an article from Gourmet Magazine about a tea shop not too far from us. We found it and enjoyed their offering.

The Howard Arms in Ilmington, between Loxley and Stratford, was a wonderful pub in a lovely village. We were the only people lunching until a couple came in. We chatted with them and they told us they were going to visit a church a short walk away accessed only by a footpath from the village and asked if we would like to join them. The Norman church is dated from the 16th Century and was restored in 1846.

Our new friends often visited the church as there were 11 mice carved in oak pews and they had not been able to find all of them. The pews and its mice were the work of Robert (Mouseman) Thompson who manufactured oak furniture.

The story goes that a conversation about "being as poor as a church mouse" took place between Thompson and a colleague during the carving of a cornice for a screen. The chance remark changed his life forever; carving a mouse remained part of his work from that time on.

Paul told me he had recently met a British couple who visited the church several times but never found all of them either.

We always knew when our day was done as Paul brushed the car against a large rosemary plant beside our parking space and the aroma signaled a collective "we're home."

Another of our daily trips was to renowned Hidcote Manor Garden. We sought shade in an area where two people were examining some trees. They told us they often travelled 50 miles "just to see these acers." Those acers were Japanese maples. They were very nice specimens, gave us shade but "50 miles and often…"

We learned of a program by local school children at a church down the road. The service closed with "Shalom." Especially pleased, Lester made a donation to the church which especially pleased and surprised the minister.

Oslo to Loxley was more than travel. Paul said it so well in an e-mail I sent asking for his recollections, "I am thankful for many things and your friendship which has been a large part of so many memories, not only on our trips together but just being together." Thank you, Paul and BettyAnn. We feel the same.

Pomp and Circumstance

As grandson Ben and his high school graduation class marched into the auditorium to Sir Edward Elgar's eponymous Pomp and Circumstance, I was reminded of an Elgar story told us at Worcester Cathedral in 1987. The year is remembered as the stock market crashed and we were in England at that time.

Lester and I entered a door in back of the cathedral. We were approached by a gentleman who asked if we would like to see the classroom where Edward Elgar had studied. Initials were carved into every desk top and he pointed out the one into which Elgar had carved his. We were equally impressed with the rare single pole vault in the middle of the room.

The gentleman further told us Elgar spent a good part of his life in Worcester. Much of his music was performed and conducted by him at the cathedral. Our time was limited so we did not see the stained glass window in the main sanctuary dedicated to him. Elgar had wished to be buried there but being a Catholic, he could not as the cathedral is part of the Church of England.

I sent an inquiry to the cathedral to confirm the story. Mr. David Morrison, librarian/archivist, responded. He had not heard about Elgar studying there. "We now know that Elgar was educated elsewhere, which makes this story extremely unlikely. However, he definitely visited the cathedral as a child." He thinks it possible the room we were in "was the Chapter House which has a pillar. Built in c.1100, it was the first round Chapter House in England." The Chapter of monks would discuss the affairs of the cathedral and monastery in that room.

Mr. Morrison: "The library and archive have been a part of the life of Worcester Cathedral since its foundation in 680." The library's collections range from medieval manuscripts and books to present day documents and archives. There is a music collection which contains the works of many famous composers, including Sir Edward Elgar.

Ben was the ninth in our family to graduate Deering High School, including his mother and me. His brother Will's graduation in three years ends the lineage as far as I can see but perhaps their mother will be writing about her grandchildren going to Deering and marching in on graduation day to Sir Edward Elgar's Pomp and Circumstance. One never knows.

Probe

As Karl and Debbie were growing up, a jigsaw puzzle was set up on a card table. Monopoly, cribbage and card games of Crazy Eights and War were ready to be played with their cousins Joe and Suzy. Probe would be played with the family around the dining room table. Probe was a word game where up to twelve letter cards were placed face down on a flat card holder and one had to guess a letter which would form a word. Three blanks could be used.

One evening after dinner, we were ready to play Probe. Earlier in the day, however, we had taken a walk in nearby woods. Aunt Helen (the children's aunt but Aunt Helen to all) spotted a pinkish flower – "pipsissewa" – and we continued our walk. Debbie's word was long: she remembered pipsissewa but Karl won with syzygy.

Jean Miller decided it would be fun to have a Winnebago, probe around and play Probe. Gasoline was $.37/gallon. Jean bought a 20-foot Winnebago. PROBE was its license plate. I drove it except for 20 minutes when Jean drove it, too nervous to drive it any longer.

Our first trip was ready. I backed out of the driveway to have the trailer hitch stop us dead in the street. It dug into soft tar. With the help of neighbors, we were freed and on our way.

We probed Williamsburg, Montreal, Quebec, the Cabot Trail, Tanglewood and Mount Desert. Staying in a camping area in Somes Sound on Mount Desert, we drove to the top of Cadillac Mountain to see the sunset and returned to see the sunrise. One morning, I sautéed mackerel on top of Cadillac Mountain. Karl had caught them the day before. Evenings were spent playing Probe.

It was decided that Probe's days for us were over when gasoline became $1.00/gallon. But because of a walk in the woods and a game after dinner, pipsissewa and Probe have not been forgotten.

Ramblings

One day during our month in Chipping Campden, Lester and I decided to go to Stow-on-the-Wold, a 16th Century market town. Some of its attached buildings were dated from that time. Most of the buildings in the town were built with Cotswold stone, a mellow beige color with a faint yellow tone.

There was a lot of activity in the large square. Morris Dancers were getting ready to perform. They were dressed alike in white pants and shirts and red suspenders. Hats were decorated with flowers and pheasant feathers and vests had hanging decorations. Strapped to their lower legs were bells affixed to black leather. They lined up and started dancing to the beat of a drum; their bells shook in unison. Sometimes they held a stick in each hand and would hit them together. Other times they waved white handkerchiefs.

They were jolly fellows who went from town to town performing. After their dancing, we asked a few if we could take their picture. They immediately put one of their hats on Lester and me and called to a fellow dancer to take a picture of all of us.

The history of Morris Dancers is sketchy. It is acknowledged they started in the 1500's as a Royal Pageant. Some insist they were a fertility myth; others, a Celtic connection. Either way, we were fortunate to find them and a lovely village.

A few years later, we were on Nantucket for a weekend. We drove around the island the first day and walked the town the next. It was noon and the town was filling up with day tourists having just arrived. We heard a familiar bell sound – Morris Dancers. They came to perform and would leave on the next ferry. Their presence took us back to Stow-on-the-Wold.

Ramblings bring delightful surprises.

Remembering Mary

Mary Sottery and I met in Portland at Nathan Clifford grammar school P.T.A. We became a committee of two to get traffic lights installed at a six-way intersection where the University of Maine Law School now sits. It is the same corner where Esther and I waited for Mr. Flaherty to go into the middle of the street, stop all traffic and yell "kee-ross" so we could scatter.

Seems as though two of Mary's boys were walking home on top of snow banks. One slipped off and got nicked by a car. Time for action. We made pests of ourselves at City Hall. Not only did we get lights, we got four-way stop signs on the street in back of the school which had five intersecting streets.

A friendship developed between us and ultimately between our families. She and Ted, a chemistry professor at the University of Maine, had three sons and a daughter. Our families would often gather for dinner. New Year's Eves were spent together with combined cooking. Mary's heritage was Greek and she would prepare something with a Greek flavor.

Mary was opinionated and political. She was elected to serve in the State Legislature. Her training as a geologist made her a natural to focus on the environment. "Protect Maine's Aquifers" became her bumper sticker battle cry. Not too many knew about aquifers, including me. She also served on the Portland City Council.

They had two camps. One was in Steuben, four hours north and east of Portland facing the sea. The other, their hunting cabin, was in the woods in South Bridgton, an hour and a half west of Portland. Mary carried a camera, never a gun. When we visited Steuben, Monopoly was immediately set up and the children had a rousing game.

One time when we were in Steuben, Mary decided we should go to Machias for Helen's famous strawberry pie. We piled into Probe and waited for Ted. Unable to decide which camera he wanted to take, he finally boarded with three cameras slung around his neck. We had pie; Ted took pictures; the children were eager to get back to Monopoly or if low tide, walk the rocks in front of the camp.

We also visited South Bridgton. Mary's old fire engine was sitting in the woods. She insisted we go to a deserted cottage so we could see its outhouse. A quarter moon was carved out of the door with "Back of the Moon" written on the door. Mary insisted we open the door. A picture of Eleanor Roosevelt stared at us. Mary had a "wicked" sense of humor.

The Sotterys had two dogs; Ted did not like cats. After their dog Mary and her daughter Baby died, Mary brought home a stray black cat. Ted took to it, named it Mavros "Greek for black but it really means marvelous." Sidney vicious, Dewey (Ellen found him near the library) and two others followed.

Thanksgiving desserts at our house were always shared with Mary and Ellen. Debbie and John took over the house when I moved to Waterville but the dessert tradition continued. When Ellen married, Mary continued alone.

Mary died last year. My fondest memory is the first time we hugged. Mary's greeting was always a handshake. Not having seen each other for several years until Ben's bar mitzvah five years ago, we shook hands. Then, we hugged. It was very moving for both of us. She was unable to make Will's bar mitzvah two years ago.

I saw Ellen after Ben's graduation this past June. She is the librarian at Deering and was there as staff. It was the first time I had seen her in five years. Her hug was lovely as were her tears.

CASTINE INN BISCUITS

4 cups flour
1 ½ tsp. salt
¼ c sugar
2 ½ tbsp. baking powder
Nutmeg
1 cup shortening

1 cup buttermilk
3 eggs, divided
¼ to ⅓ cup water

Beaten egg

400 degree oven

Combine dry ingredients. Cut in shortening.

Combine buttermilk, two eggs, ¼ cup water. Stir into above. Add more water if needed just to hold the dough together.

Place dough on parchment paper; pat out to ½ inch. Cut into diamonds and place on parchment paper lined cookie tray. Brush with beaten egg. Bake 15 minutes or until nicely browned.

Reheat in oven, NOT microwave.

Note: The Castine Inn in Castine, Maine serves these biscuits directly from the oven. They were so good I asked for the recipe which they gave me without hesitation. The recipe had been printed up so evidently many people asked for it. We have enjoyed them at home directly from the oven for many years. Using Kosher salt in all my cooking, I do use a little salt. The amount given is the amount in the recipe for Castine Inn Biscuits.

DOWN EAST FISH CHOWDER

1 onion, diced
Butter

2 potatoes, peeled and diced
Water
Salt
Pepper

1 pound haddock

Sautée onion in butter until transparent.

Add potatoes; cover with water; add salt and pepper. Cook until potatoes are done.

Place haddock on top of potatoes and cook through. Break up haddock.

Cheese sauce:

2 tbsp. butter
2 tbsp. flour

1 cup milk

6 tbsp. extra sharp cheddar cheese cut into small pieces.

Cook flour in melted butter, stirring, for 2 minutes. Gradually add milk, stirring. Add cheese; stir and simmer to boiling.

Stir cheese sauce into chowder.

Ruby and Kate

Brownies were successfully sold at a restaurant in Portland. I thought I would try to expand the sale of them and other sweets as well.

The name of a small restaurant, Ruby Begonia, intrigued me. It was in Portland's Old Port area which was developing with restaurants, boutique and antique shops, gift shops, etc. I telephoned asking if I could bring a sampling of sweets which would include brownies, carrot cake and linzer tarts. A time to meet with the manager was arranged.

And so I met Kate, an ebullient young woman. She was also bartender. We talked about the sweets over the offered cold drink. It was her feeling that homemade sweets would be very nice. She would talk it over with the owner.

As we continued to talk, I sensed something special about Kate. I said I would love for her to meet my daughter Debbie who I felt would benefit from her enthusiastic manner. They met and that was the start of a friendship that continues, 31 years later. I have been her surrogate mom those same years.

Pritham Singh, owner of Ruby Begonia, lived nearby and agreed to pick up the sweets. After a couple of pick-ups, I thought quiche cooling on the table where his sweets were waiting for him might pique his interest as quiche was not on the menu. They did and spinach quiche and mushroom quiche became part of Ruby's fare.

As fall approached, business slowed, I was not being paid though I continued to bake and was delivering. The last time I saw Pritham Singh was when I waited an hour and a half for him to appear at Ruby Begonia so I could collect the $400.00 awarded to me by Small Claims court. He gave me a check which I immediately cashed. He ultimately became successful in revitalization of Portland and in real estate development in the Florida Keys.

Kate in recent years has been writing cookbooks. "Wild Maine Recipes" includes cooking with beaver, moose, venison, rabbit and other exotic meats. The last time I saw her was in June at a family lunch after grandson Ben's high school graduation. Though struggling with pain from recent back surgery, she was still my Kate. She told me she finally made linzer tarts.

LINZER TARTS

1 cup unsalted butter, softened
⅔ cup sugar
1 ¼ cup ground almonds
1 ¾ cup flour
1 tsp. vanilla

Raspberry preserves
Confectioners' sugar

Cream butter and sugar very well. Add almonds, flour and vanilla to make a smooth dough.

Roll out between ⅛ and ¼ inch thick. Cut with cookie cutter into an equal number of rounds. Cut the centers out of half the rounds (a thimble works well.) Place on a cookie tray lined with parchment paper.

Bake in a 350 degree oven 10 minutes or until lightly browned. Cool. Spread whole cookies with raspberry preserves. Cover tops with confectioners' sugar and place on top of whole cookie.

Serve Me First

I arrived at a lovely home set back from the road. It was approached by a long drive, a duck pond, a riding corral with a white split rail fence and a horse stable. Mrs. Davis greeted me as I brought food into the house for a cocktail party, coffee and sweets. "We own Shaw's, you know." She saw supplies in Hannaford bags. I marketed at Hannaford as it was closer to my home. Dale, its produce manager, selected choice fruit and vegetables for me, so critical in catering. I told Mrs. Davis I did not know they owned Shaw's and thought to myself this is the last time here. It turned out not to be so.

Arriving a second time with lunch for a visiting English family, the foods, including Dale's produce, were in Shaw's bags which did not go unnoticed by Mrs. Davis.

Having to go through the den to get to the sunroom where lunch was to be served, I noticed world maps on the walls. They had been marked up indicating where the Davis's had been. Also in the den were Mr. Davis's riding boots. Mr. Davis told me he rode every day and he had to have hip surgery. I asked him if he would be able to ride after surgery: "Wouldn't have it if I couldn't."

My last job with them was a dinner party for eight which I would serve. Mrs. Davis gave me instructions for serving: "You will serve me first and then serve to my right. Plates would be cleared the same way." I knew serve left, clear right but something told me to check further. "Home Makers Guide," written by Marjorie Standish and published in 1929, was a book I had picked up for no particular reason other than reading about the way things used to be. It had the information I needed: "The hostess is often served first." I couldn't resist telling Mrs. Davis I had done my homework. There has been no need for the book since.

CHICKEN SALAD

4 large chicken breasts

½ bottle Catalina dressing
½ tsp. thyme
Salt
Pepper
Salad Dressing (Miracle Whip)
Green grapes, halved
Sliced almonds
Butter

Poach skinless chicken breasts or bake them with skins on, salted and peppered. Remove from liquid when done, cool; remove skins if baked; cut into chunks. Place in bowl.

Pour Catalina Dressing over chicken and mix with salt, pepper and dried thyme. Combine well, using more dressing if necessary to coat chicken. Refrigerate an hour or so until chicken absorbs the dressing.

Stir in enough additional Miracle Whip to moisten; stir in grapes and almonds which have been sautéed in a little butter.

Make a day in advance of serving.

Note: Amounts are not critical in this recipe. I would not use mayonnaise as the salad dressing complements the Catalina Dressing.

STRAWBERRY SOUP

1 ½ cups water
¾ cup red wine
½ cup sugar
2 tbsp. lemon juice
1 cinnamon stick
1 quart strawberries, stemmed and puréed

½ cup whipping cream
¼ cup sour cream

Combine water, wine, sugar, lemon juice and cinnamon stick. Boil uncovered 15 minutes, stirring occasionally. Add strawberry purée and boil, stirring frequently, 10 minutes or more. Discard cinnamon stick. Cool.

Whip cream. Combine with sour cream and fold into strawberry mixture.

Serve at cool room temperature.

Tea For Two

Cooking classes were offered at a gourmet shop in Portland. I could teach classes of my choosing. In the cooking area at the back of the shop, there was a large overhead mirror where the demonstrations took place. I did like some hands on during the class. Some were eager to help while others were there to take notes and taste.

A class on the traditional English cream tea was offered and attended to capacity. We were to have cucumber and watercress sandwiches, smoked salmon sandwiches, scones, lemon curd, clotted cream and preserves.

As the scones were baking, I made up the lemon curd as it required constant stirring to prevent curdling. Volunteers removed crusts and buttered breads. Others made the sandwiches. The tea was brewed using loose tea. When people signed up for the class, I requested they bring a cup and saucer. It was time to indulge in a cream tea.

As I was cleaning up, an elderly gentleman came up to me, thanked me for the class and said he had enjoyed it immensely. "This is the first cooking class I have attended and I came because of my love for the English tea. I have been to London 23 times and always have tea at Brown's. I am going in three weeks – would you come with me?"

LEMON CURD

⅓ cup butter
1 cup sugar
2 lemons, juice and rind
3 eggs, slightly beaten.

Combine all in a saucepan. Stir constantly with a wooden spoon over low heat until mixture is hot (NOT BOILING) and thick. Pour into container. Cool. Cover. Refrigerate. Will thicken more when refrigerated. Keeps for a week.

SCONES

4 cups flour
2 tsp. baking powder
2 tbsp. sugar
Pinch salt
1 ½ sticks butter, softened
2 tbsp. raisins
2 eggs, lightly beaten
Milk to mix

400 degree oven. Parchment paper lined cookie trays. Bake about 20 minutes.

Combine dry ingredients into mixing bowl.

Cut butter into dry ingredients until resembling breadcrumbs. Add raisins. Add eggs and combine. Add milk a little at a time until mixture becomes a ball of dough.

Pat out on floured board ½ inch thick and cut into squares or diamonds. Place on cookie trays. Bake until nicely browned.

That's a Jean Miller

Having been willed Jean Miller's collection of her intricately cut stencils and those of George Lord, the "Portland Chair Painter" of the mid 1800's, I felt they belonged in the Maine State Museum for their historic value and proper care. Jean DeLand Miller decorated by graining, stenciling and freehand bronze, a technique allowing one to use a colored background as opposed to a black background as for stenciling. A design was painted on the object with black varnish and when it became "tacky," the same bronzing powders were applied. Coloring the decoration in both techniques was the same. The freehand bronze item, however, had to be antiqued. Everything was varnished.

In the mid 1800's, George Lord grained and stenciled furniture for Cory Co. in Portland. Cory Co. was a pioneer in manufactured furniture. Ultimately, C.A. Pierce of Pierce Furniture decorated furniture "using the Lord stencils" as indicated on his billheads. When Mr. Pierce was no longer able to decorate, he knew of Jean's decorating and he turned to her. He gave her the Lord stencils and she continued to stencil for Mr. Pierce.

Jean learned to cut stencils and to stencil at Portland night school. Freehand bronze was touched upon but she developed it into a viable decorating tool. Using her stencils and some of Lord's, she established her own decorating business. Many years later, she taught me to stencil and do freehand bronze. There was no need for me to cut stencils as she had hers and Lord's.

The gift of the stencils to the Maine State Museum filled a void in their decorated collection. They were delighted as they could now make them available for research. Also included in the gift was a freehand bronze decorated spice box containing six individual boxes. Each was decorated differently. In his thank you letter to me, Curator Churchill told me that when he had a Board meeting to talk about the acquisition, one member upon entering the meeting saw the spice box and said, "That's a Jean Miller."

I retained a few stencils with the intent of turning them over to the Museum which I did a few years later. At that time, the staff was involved in cataloguing hundreds of newly acquired stencils. They were the stencils of the teacher that Jean had at Portland night school.

In the final thank you, the Museum asked if they could keep the box in which I brought the stencils (a plastic box used for fish deliveries at stores) as they did not have one in their collection of boxes...

AMBROSIA JEAN MILLER

1 pound lobster, cooked, cut up
1 pound haddock, cooked, broken up

1 recipe cream sauce made with 1/2 and 1/2 cream
3 tbsp. sherry

Town House crackers

Butter

350 degree oven. Buttered casserole. 30 minutes.

Combine lobster and haddock in casserole.

Make cream sauce; stir in sherry. Pour over lobster and haddock; stir to combine.

Cover top with cracker crumbs. Dot with butter. Bake until bubbly.

The Blueberry Pie Gang

The gang was mostly family at Little Sebago. They numbered 18 today and were waiting for blueberry pie and, I suppose, to see Lester and me, the bearers of the blueberry pies.

My blueberry pie is never picture perfect. The edges of the top crust have several places where the cooking blueberry juices leak through and all over the edges onto the foil-lined pan waiting for them. It happens every time as I cannot resist over-filling the pie with the blueberries. The years have prepared me to address leakage. The edges of the crust are a little thick; however, there has never been crust left on plates as it is well done, flaky and delicious.

The blueberries are not the restaurant thick set stuff or "goop" as Connie calls it. No, they are runny and a perfect slice is impossible. Not a very pretty blueberry pie but it doesn't matter because as everyone ate their warm blueberry pie, they knew that nestled in with those little Maine gems was the love for them that makes my blueberry pie so special.

BLUEBERRY PANCAKES

1 cup flour
2 tsp sugar
¾ tsp. baking powder
Pinch salt

1 cup buttermilk, room temperature
1 egg, room temperature
2 tbsp. butter, melted

1/3 cup blueberries, fresh or frozen

Combine dry ingredients in medium size bowl.

Combine buttermilk, egg and melted butter. Stir into dry ingredients. Stir in blueberries.

Canola oil

Brush frying pan with Canola oil; heat on moderate heat until oil sizzles with a sprinkle of water. Add 2 heaping tbsp. batter or desired amount for each pancake. Cook until browned on one side; flip pancakes and cook until browned. Takes less time on second side. Brush pan with oil before each batch of pancakes. Keep warm in 200 degree oven until all are made. Serve with blueberry sauce or maple syrup. Makes about 10.

BLUEBERRY SAUCE

2 cups blueberries
3 tbsp. water
2-3 tbsp. sugar or to taste
Dash cinnamon
Lemon juice, if desired

1 tbsp. cornstarch
2 tbsp. water

In small saucepan, bring berries, water, cinnamon and lemon juice to a boil, stirring occasionally, until berries are mostly cooked. Some should remain whole but softened.

Dissolve cornstarch in water to make a slurry. Slowly add to boiling berries, stirring, until desired thickness. May not take all the cornstarch.

BLUEBERRY PIE

1 recipe pâte brisée

6 cups blueberries
Lemon juice (optional)

½ cup flour
1 cup sugar
Cinnamon

Butter
Cream
Sugar

400 degree oven. 9 inch pie plate.

Mix flour and sugar and a couple dashes cinnamon.

Place blueberries in bowl; add flour sugar mixture and mix well. Add lemon juice.

Roll out a little more than half the pâte brisée. Place in pie plate. Add blueberries.
Dot with butter.

Roll out top crust; place on blueberries; crimp edges. Make several slits on top.

Brush with cream; sprinkle lightly with sugar.

Place on a foil-lined pan. Bake. If top is browning too fast, lay a piece of foil on top
of the pie. Oven temperature can be lowered to 375 degrees if pie is cooking too fast.
Top should be browned when done.

Note: Frozen Maine blueberries work well. Do not defrost.

ESTHER'S BLUEBERRY STREUSEL MUFFINS

2 cups flour
2 ½ tsp. baking powder
½ tsp. baking soda
¼ cup sugar
½ tsp. grated nutmeg

6 tbsp. butter, melted
1 egg
1 cup low-fat yoghurt or buttermilk
1 tbsp. vanilla
1 cup fresh or frozen (not defrosted) blueberries

Streusel Topping:

¼ cup butter, softened
½ cup flour
½ cup sugar
½ tsp. almond extract (optional)
¼ cup sliced almonds

Oven 375 degrees. Bake 20 minutes in muffin tin lined with muffin papers.

Combine dry ingredients.

Combine liquids and blueberries. Stir into dry ingredients.

Divide batter into muffin tin.

Combine streusel topping and sprinkle on each muffin. Bake.

Cool muffins in tin 5 minutes. Turn muffin on sides in tin to cool completely.

The Holy Four

Many years ago, ten of us went to Nice for a week. We had talked about going and decided it was time as Donald was struggling with cancer. Paul wrote to a former Norwegian teaching colleague for a suggestion where to stay. She recommended the Star Hotel where she and her husband had stayed. I was put in charge of making reservations as we had a fax. We were ready to go.

The hotel worked out well. We gathered over croissants and café au lait to discuss the day and we were off. The old city was within walking distance.

After two days, Joanna decided we should hire a car with a driver. Next morning, a van picked us up and we were on our way to a market town in Italy known to Claire and Carmen. We went separate ways, agreeing to meet at a specific time. When we got into the van, the driver asked, "Would you like to go to Dolceacqua for lunch? Monet painted there." The idea of being where Monet painted was overwhelming to me.

We had lunch al fresco, facing the medieval fortress of the Andrea Doria family and the rib-vaulted bridge with its plaque indicating Monet had painted there in 1884. The painting, Bridge at Dolceacqua, is in the Sterling and Francine Clark Art Institute in Williamstown, Massachusetts. A member of the Doria family built the fortress in the 16th Century. It is the same family named for the SS Andrea Doria ocean liner which sank off Nantucket in 1956.

We decided we should have the van another day. We would go to the Matisse Chapel in Vence. We got there and it was closed. We had visited Matisse's home in Nice but it would have been wonderful to have seen what he considered to be his masterpiece. "How would you like to visit Renoir's home in Cagne-sur-Mer?" My word, this driver was a gift. The home was surrounded by olive trees and was a museum. We were actually in Renoir's studio with his brushes, paints, paint-covered palette, easel and wheelchair.

After the visit to Renoir's home, we were on our way to the town of Cagne-sur-Mer for the rest of the afternoon. "A Picasso Museum is just up there," our driver said, pointing it out to us. We returned to the Star after another splendid day.

At this point, Paul realized he needed money and went into a bank. When he came out, he told us how embarrassed he was when getting his travelers checks and passport out of his trouser pocket. He kept both in his pocket which he kept secured with a safety pin from the inside of his trousers. The rest of his money he kept in his sock. No gypsies would rob him.

As we were nearing time to leave Nice, we realized we hadn't had bouillabaisse. That was remedied by going to an alley full of restaurants where we could eat al fresco. Lester and I shared a huge serving of bouillabaisse brought to us in the pot in which it was cooked. We enjoyed it immensely.

Lunch our last day in Nice was to be a splurge at the five-star Hotel Negresco which was across the street from the renowned Nice beach. Our reservation found us in a room away from the dining room. Champagne was ordered to celebrate the occasion and the wonderful time we had being together. Lunch was brought in by the waiters who were followed by six men in white gloves and black uniforms. Our lunches, covered by large domes, were placed in front of us. The gloved personnel had placed themselves between us; on cue, they removed the domes, lifting them into the air in a sweeping motion to reveal the smallest serving of food ever experienced in a restaurant. We taxied back to our Star and took a nap to get ready for couscous in a restaurant next door to the hotel.

Years later, Paul, BettyAnn, Lester and I had lunch at the Savoy in London. Lamb was carved table side and served with potatoes and vegetables. Pudding rounded out the lovely lunch. Of course we compared it to lunch at the Negresco.

There is no doubt being in the shadows of Monet, Matisse, Renoir and Picasso was for me the ultimate experience of our trip to Nice.

Three Muses

Sophie spoke Greek to me through her teachings – how to bake, how to sew, how to be more tolerant. Friends for more than 50 years, we shared our growing families with outings at Two Lights State Park in Cape Elizabeth where she would often grill swordfish which had marinated in lemon juice, olive oil and oregano. As she grilled, she kept her four children in order. Fourth of July was often spent in the park. Sophie and I would leave for a while to pick strawberries nearby.

"You have to beat the butter until it is white" was what she taught me in making frenekia, koulourakia and paxamadakia. Though no butter to beat, we made the ultimate Greek pastry, baklava.

Sophie taught me to sew, a gift from her tailor father and one that came naturally to me as my grandfather was a tailor. Her mother embroidered all the window shades in their home. Her gift from her mother was in the form of oil and watercolor painting.

She also shared her friend Hélène. She, too, was a wonderful cook but it was her wisdom that fed my soul.

Both women suffered the loss of a child. Yet, they exhibited grace and dignity to all who shared their grief. Their lessons in so many ways were gifts to me from the ages.

Spanakopita. I turned to Xenia who I knew as our daughters were best friends. She had a Greek restaurant nearby and was pleased to help. "The spinach (frozen) is to be washed with hot water until the water runs clear and the water to be squeezed out until the spinach is dry." Cheeses, eggs, a little minced onion were mixed in. Phyllo was buttered and ready for the spinach mixture. It was cut, baked to a beautiful brown and ready to be devoured with a Greek salad including some iceberg lettuce as instructed by Hélène.

Xenia's spanakopita became my "signature dish" in catering. Making it as an hors d'oeuvre or part of the entrée, it was served at most every party I catered.

KOULOURAKIA

1 ½ sticks butter, softened
⅓ cup shortening
1 cup sugar
3 eggs, divided
2 ½ tbsp. milk
1 tsp. vanilla
3 tbsp. whiskey
¼ cup orange juice

4 cups flour
2 tsp. baking powder
½ tsp. baking soda
¼ tsp. cinnamon
¼ tsp. nutmeg
½ tsp. salt
Sesame seeds

350 degree oven. Parchment paper lined cookie trays.

Beat butter and shortening very well. Add sugar gradually, beating well. Beat in 2 eggs, one at a time; add liquids.

Combine dry ingredients; add to above. Shape. Place on cookie trays. Bake 20 minutes or until browned.

To Shape: Break off a piece of dough. Form into an 8 inch rope. Twist. Fold in half. Brush with beaten egg; sprinkle with sesame seeds.

Two Gracious Women

As a docent at Colby Museum of Art several years ago, when told we were to write a paper on an artist in the permanent collection, I immediately decided my paper would be on a Maine woman artist. It was easy for me to select Beverly Hallam and her painting "Violins."

Beverly and her friend Mary-Leigh Smart shared their love of art, Mary-Leigh having donated "Violins" to Colby. Lester and I had the pleasure of meeting them at a Colby luncheon. Hugh Gourley, Director of the Museum, arranged with Beverly for three staff members and me to visit Beverly's studio. It was at their home by the sea in York. It was magical visiting the studio half of the house which Beverly occupied and Mary-Leigh's half filled with Beverly's and other artists' work. When Beverly and Mary-Leigh came to visit a show at the museum, they shared lunch at our home together with some museum staff.

A consummate artist, Beverly was the first to use acrylics, creating large paintings of flowers she usually grew. She photographed her arrangements from all angles, while remembering Renoir's words to Matisse: "When I have arranged a bouquet in order to paint it, I go around to the side I have not looked at."

It is, however, the future these two gracious women have carved out that I want to share.

They have established the Surf Point Foundation, an artists' colony to be created on the 42-acre oceanfront property belonging to Mary-Leigh. Their plan started in the late 1980's and became a reality in November, 2007 when a York Land Trust easement was obtained to prevent the land from being developed.

The idea of the artists' colony came from the MacDowell Colony in New Hampshire which created retreats for artists, writers, musicians to create in a private atmosphere away from the public. The MacDowell Colony hosted the likes of Leonard Bernstein, Willa Cather and Studs Terkel. Thornton Wilder worked on "Our Town" during his stay there. Each unit of the Surf Point Foundation Colony will include a sleeping space, kitchenette and large studio space. It will be provided for a year to each recipient.

Upon the death of Mary-Leigh, the plans for this artists' colony will go into effect with seven studios and a residence for the colony's director. An old home on the property where May Sarton lived for 22 years will have four studios. Beverly's studio, living quarters, extensive library and assets will go to the Foundation upon her death.

It is difficult to think of these two vibrant women in terms of their deaths. And yet, they have clearly thought about it. Their love of art, as well as the protection of the land, will be their legacy. In addition, there will be the gift of Beverly's art.

Carl Little, in his book, "Beverly Hallam: An Odyssey in Art," tells the following story as told him by Mrs. Hallam who was a hairdresser: Alice Hallam related meeting Leonard Bernstein's father Sam who sold hairdressing supplies. One day they got talking about their kids. "You can't imagine what my son Lennie wants to be. He wants to be a composer…of music…a musician! Can you believe it? I can't stand it." He then asked Alice what her daughter wanted to do. "She is going to be an artist," Beverly's mother proudly answered. "Oh my God," Bernstein replied, "they're both going to starve to death!"

We Will Serve Cholent

Before our friends retired, scattered and left us, we thought a horse drawn sleigh ride would be fun. There were 12 of us. The sleigh turned out to be a cart. Hampered by lack of snow, we got stuck in mud. We didn't care as we were good friends. Donald's libations kept us warm and happy.

Lunch would be at our home after the ride. In discussing what to serve, Lester said, "We will serve cholent." I had never cooked cholent nor tasted it. Lester raved about his mother's cholent. I was reminded when I was speaking with a client and she asked if I made chopped liver: "Does your mother make chopped liver?" "She makes the best chopped liver." "No, I don't make chopped liver." I did not want to tempt the fates then but tempt them I must for cholent.

Cholent is a Jewish dish of central European origin: meat, potatoes, lima or navy beans, barley, onions, molasses, garlic, salt and pepper. It is baked in a very low oven and placed in the oven before sundown on Friday. It was to be ready for the Jewish Sabbath when cooking was not allowed by Orthodox Jews. It was served as lunch. Dessert would be an afternoon nap. My family adhered to the nap after lunch but my mother never made cholent.

Just in case the cholent was a disaster as it was unheard of by our friends, we had hot dogs and their accouterment. I made assorted cookies to serve with fruit for dessert. The cholent was a success and all went home for an afternoon nap.

What Do You Want

This is how the Alfond Youth Center YMCA Day Camp Tracy in Oakland, Maine began, grew and presently is.

"In the 1960's George Keller, Executive Director of the YMCA, asked Richard Hawkes, President of a local bank and me, Lester Jolovitz (a local lawyer), to go with him to view land owned by Mona Tracy who wanted to sell her 64 acres of woods leading to McGrath Pond, known locally as McGraw Pond. George had three hatchets in the trunk of his car and the three of us in business suits hacked our way through the woods to the water. It was beautiful and we had no doubts as to the potential of the land for a children's camp."

George Keller came to Waterville in the late 1950's as Director of the YMCA with the mission to open the "Y" to children and families of all denominations. His peaceful gentle nature was in perfect keeping with his adopted Quaker religion and its traditions of equality, justice and pacifism. Lester said of him: "George was respected and admired. He had complete integrity. There were no maybes – he called it as it was. He was modest and had no political aspirations. He was not a man of wealth or power."

There were three stipulations for the YMCA to buy the Tracy land: it was to be at a discounted rate, a cash exchange, and the Tracy name would be kept. The 64 acres were deeded to the YMCA on March 29, 1968 and partially used as a summer day camp with eight week programs. Buildings for recreation, changing rooms and daily activities were put up.

In the meantime, Ken Walsh came to the Waterville Boys & Girls Club as Director in 1992. Shortly after his arrival, he was taken to meet philanthropist Harold Alfond at Harold's home. Ken recalls: "The Patriots were playing and Drew Bledsoe was their quarterback. The game had Harold's attention and after Bledsoe scored a touchdown, he turned to me and said, 'What do you want.' I told him I wanted money and lots of it. Harold offered $50,000 with a five-year challenge or a one-to-one challenge up to $500,000. We chose the one-to-one challenge and raised $2.1 million in the community to renovate the Boys & Girls Club."

In 1994, playing golf with Harold in Palm Beach, Ken indicated to Harold that all the entities, i.e., Boys & Girls Club, YMCA and Parks and Recreation Department were vying for the same money. Harold: "What would it take to pull the three entities together?" Ken: "Lots of money." Thus began the seed that grew to become the Alfond Youth Center, a combination of the Boys & Girls Club and YMCA under one roof, the only facility of its kind in the country.

In 1998, discussions began to merge the three entities with Harold's backing. There was to be no debt. The YMCA was $800,000 in debt and would sell 32 acres of the Tracy land. Camp Tracy with its 32 acres would be turned over to the Alfond Youth Center. The $500,000 endowment of the Boys & Girls Club would also be turned over to The Alfond Youth Center. True to his word, Harold Alfond donated a sum to be challenged. The challenge was met and the Alfond Youth Center was dedicated in May, 1999 by Senator George Mitchell, a Waterville native who spent many early years with his brothers at the Boys Club. Colin Powell visited the facility in October as a representative of America's Resources.

George Keller died in September, 2001. Lester paid tribute to his friend by establishing the George Keller Foundation Scholarship which awards $500 on a yearly basis to an applicant towards his/her first college semester. The applicants must submit a paper on how George's values have impacted their lives.

Camp Tracy began to flourish with a $1 million challenge by the New Balance Foundation to build a four seasons lodge among other facilities. The Unity Foundation gave a $150,000 grant to build three cabins which were first occupied by 31 Chinese students who came to Maine for three weeks to learn English. Part of the $2 million campaign went for tennis courts, a waterfront lodge, the four seasons lodge, a bath house, outdoor theater, rope course, climbing wall, hiking trails and the Harold Alfond Fenway Park baseball field which is a story unto itself.

Baseball was a strong influence in Ken's youth, playing it with his brothers in cornfields in upstate New York. Knowing Harold was a baseball fanatic too, Ken shared his dream with Harold to replicate Fenway Park in the two-tiered ball field at Camp Tracy. "If you call it Fenway Park, I'll give you the money." Ken refused Harold's offer, feeling it was time to give back. "It will be our pleasure to give something to you."

Gardner Savings Bank contributed $100,000, the Red Sox Foundation, $50,000 and Cal Ripken, Jr. Foundation, $50,000. There were additional donors. Ken worked out the legalities for using the name Fenway Park which led to the 2/3 replica of the Park. Harold Alfond Fenway Park was dedicated September 9, 2009 by Cal Ripken, Jr., Dr. John Winkin and Governor John Baldacci.

The Heritage Circle comprises major contributors to the Alfond Youth Center. In the summer of 2009, Lester and I attended a Heritage Circle meeting at Camp Tracy. We watched campers do skits on an old wooden platform. Lester asked Ken what happened when it rained. The answer was obvious. Something needed to be done.

Steve Aucoin, a building entrepreneur who worked for the Alfond Youth Center, came for lunch with Ken and plans were drawn up to construct a theater on the idea of the "shell" used by the Boston Pops. There would be excellent acoustics, dressing rooms, stage lights, back stair entry and a roof to keep performers dry. It would be handicapped accessible. July 30, 2010, the Jolovitz Outdoor Theater was dedicated.

Camp Tracy continues to grow, fueled by the energy, ideas and ideals of Ken Walsh. This August there will be two overnight baseball camps. Baseball legends, including Tommy John and Mike Torrez, will be helping the young players. Included in the staff are CIT's – Coaches in Training. One of the coaches in training is our 15-year-old grandson Will. In the tradition of his grandfather, Will is donating his week to Camp Tracy.

White Perch

Lester's former secretary Ruth delivered white perch Wayne caught the day before. Wayne's white perch came as skinned fillets.

I was reminded of rowing my grandfather around Field's Pond in Orrington. He fished for white perch and, hopefully, a pickerel. My grandparents had a camp on the water side of the pond: no water, no electricity and we had to get there by rowboat. When there was serious white perch fishing, the family would get into two rowboats. With only one motor, we would grasp the second boat and go in tandem to "the rock." "The rock" was a large rock jutting into the pond on the opposite side. Fishing there was good until an eel or hornpout was caught. My grandfather would then declare "fishing's over." We would tandem back to the camp and clean the fish. My grandmother cooked them. From childhood, we were cautioned about the bones in white perch.

We used to row by the Shiro cottage, a point of reference on the land side of the Pond. We always talked about how nice it would be to have a cottage on the land side where there was water, electricity and we could drive up to the door. Aunt Rose and Uncle Abe made it possible. They bought the Shiro cottage. Years ago, Debbie and her cousin Joe went to the cottage for a couple of days' fishing. Debbie said: "We caught and then cleaned 52 white perch until two in the morning. They were iced for Joe to take back to Florida." Grandson Ben has fished Field's Pond. He kept yellow perch. First time anyone in the family had kept them. Debbie said they were good.

Lester has talked about rowing his father around a lake to catch white perch which were always biting better "over there." The catch was gifted to his mother to clean. There were always enough for his father to give away to his friends.

My Uncle Edwin and his family summered at Little Sebago. He loved to fish for white perch. He bargained with me. He'd catch; I'd clean. Wayne's white perch got me thinking about my uncle's bargain. Cleaning meant scaling, gutting and cutting off the heads. They were then ready to be floured and fried in butter. White perch were not sautéed.

Ben loves to fish off the dock at Little Sebago but he does not keep what he catches.

It should be noted that except for Ben's catch at Field's Pond, none of us ever kept a yellow perch. Until then, we were exclusively a white perch family.

Yum Yum

A client called asking me to cater a party. They had moved from Cape Elizabeth to Cumberland on the Greely Road, a lovely country road with open fields where sheep, cattle and horses grazed.

The party was set up and I was asked if I would like to see their sheep. After viewing them, I asked if they ate them. "Oh, yes. They are all named Yum Yum."

STILTON WALNUT TORTA

1 8-ounce package cream cheese, room temperature
½ cup butter, room temperature

2 tbsp. sherry

¼ pound Stilton, crumbled

¼ cup walnuts, coarsely chopped

Walnut halves

Red grapes
Crackers

1 quart bowl, lined with plastic wrap.

Beat butter and cream cheese until light. Add sherry and mix.

Spread half cream cheese mixture in bowl. Press half of Stilton into cream cheese mixture. Sprinkle with half of walnuts. Repeat.

Cover with plastic wrap, pressing down to eliminate air pockets. Refrigerate.

Place plate on top of torta. Invert. Remove plastic and smooth with knife.

Garnish with walnut halves around the bottom if desired. Serve with Carr crackers and grapes. Recipe can be doubled.

SWEET AND SOUR MEATBALLS

Meatballs:

1 pound hamburger
1 onion, grated
1 egg
¼ cup bread crumbs
Salt
Pepper
Garlic powder

Mix. Make into cocktail size meatballs.

Sauce:

¾ cup chili sauce
¼ cup grape jelly
½ cup water
Juice of 1 lemon

Cook until jelly dissolves; drop in meatballs. Simmer 1 hour.

About the Author

I am a lifelong Mainer…well, almost. In the beginning, there was a three year hiatus in Springfield, Massachusetts, where my twin sister and I joined our parents and sister. We then moved to Portland, Maine, where I grew up. After college, there was a two year hiatus in Boston where my son Karl was born. We returned to Portland where my daughter Deborah was born on our – remember, I am a twin – 25th birthday. To put years aside and age to rest, I will be 77 in May.

Although a self-taught cook, I accepted Julia Child's teaching when she charged onto the television screen. I was able to master the art of her French cooking which together with Greek cooking shared by friends, English cooking learned from family and Jewish cooking ingrained from my heritage, I had a repertoire ready to be marketed. And I did.

I catered for many years in the Portland area, taught adult education in Portland and Cape Elizabeth and provided food demonstrations at the Whip and Spoon gourmet shop in Portland and the Stern's Department Store in Waterville.

Lester Jolovitz from Waterville appeared on the scene 28 years ago at a bar mitzvah I catered in Portland and soon after I was part of the Waterville culture. Always interested in art, I became a docent at Colby Museum of Art.

Together, Lester and I are Zayde and Bubbe (grandfather and grandmother) to Ben, Will and Nicky and several of our dear, caring younger friends. Sadly, Lester died February 29th, 2012. His memory lives on through Reminiscences and Recipes.

Barbara Rogers Jolovitz
April, 2012.